# 2010 Supplement

# FEDERAL
# INCOME TAXATION OF
# BUSINESS
# ORGANIZATIONS

FOURTH EDITION

*by*

PAUL R. MCDANIEL
Professor of Law and
James J. Freeland Eminent Scholar in Taxation
University of Florida

MARTIN J. MCMAHON, JR.
Stephen C. O'Connell Professor of Law
University of Florida

DANIEL L. SIMMONS
Professor of Law
University of California at Davis

NEW YORK, NEW YORK
**FOUNDATION PRESS**
2010

© 2010 By THOMSON REUTERS/FOUNDATION PRESS

       1 New York Plaza, 34th Floor
       New York, NY 10004
       Phone Toll Free 1–877–888–1330
       Fax (646) 424–5201
       foundation–press.com

Printed in the United States of America

**ISBN** 978–1–59941–815–5

Mat #40975419

# PREFACE

This 2010 Supplement to Federal Income Taxation of Business Organizations provides users of the text with materials reflecting developments in federal income taxation of corporations and partnerships since January 31, 2006 (the date as of which the materials in the text are current). This supplement is current as of July 1, 2010 and includes all significant federal income tax legislation, Treasury Regulations, judicial decisions, and Internal Revenue Service rulings promulgated after January 31, 2006 and before July 1, 2010.

Portions of the updates in this Supplement are derived from the current developments outline produced by Martin McMahon, Ira Shepard and Daniel Simmons. We gratefully acknowledge Professor Shepard's contribution to the materials in this supplement.

PAUL R. MCDANIEL
MARTIN J. MCMAHON, JR.
DANIEL L. SIMMONS

July 1, 2010

# TABLE OF CONTENTS

# TABLE OF INTERNAL REVENUE CODE SECTIONS

# TABLE OF TREASURY REGULATIONS

## PROPOSED TREASURY REGULATIONS

# TABLE OF CASES AND RULINGS

References are to Pages.

2010 Supplement

# FEDERAL INCOME TAXATION OF BUSINESS ORGANIZATIONS

# PART I

# TAXATION OF PARTNERS AND PARTNERSHIPS

## CHAPTER 1

## INTRODUCTION TO PARTNERSHIP TAXATION

### SECTION 2. DEFINITION OF A PARTNERSHIP

### A. PARTNERSHIP VERSUS OTHER BUSINESS ARRANGEMENT

**Page 5:**

**In the fourth full paragraph, at the end of the third full sentence, add the following footnote 4A:**

4A. Treas. Reg. § 301.7701-3(b)(1) treats an unincorporated entity with only a single owner (generally only an LLC), as a disregarded entity. The single owner is treated as owning directly all of the assets of the entity and is thus taxed directly on the entity's activities. This aspect of the regulations was upheld in Littriello v. United States, 484 F.3d 372 (6th Cir. 2007) and McNamee v. Department of the Treasury, 488 F.3d 100 (2d Cir. 2007).

**Page 13.**

**After the heading,** *"1.3 Husband and Wife Partnerships"*, **insert:**

Section 761(f), added in 2007, provides that a husband and wife who operate a qualified joint venture may elect not to treat the joint venture as a partnership. A qualified joint venture is one conducted by a husband and wife, both of whom are material participants, and who file a joint return. Each spouse is required to report the spouse's share of income and expense items on a separate schedule C. Each spouse is individually assessed self-employment tax. I.R.C. § 1402(a)(17), as amended by the 2007 Act.

**Page 14;**

**At the end of the first full paragraph, insert:**

See Rev. Rul. 2004-77, 2004-2 C.B. 119.

**Page 22:**

**After the second full paragraph, insert:**

Several recent decisions have disregarded purported partnership arrangements in abusive tax shelter cases. The courts have tended to deny the sought-after tax benefits by finding that there was no valid partnership, rather than analyzing the transactions as lacking economic substance. For example, TIFD III-E, Inc. v. United States, 459 F.3d 220 (2d Cir. 2006), (commonly referred to as the *Castle Harbour* case) involved a tax shelter partnership in which 2 percent of both operating and taxable income was allocated to GECC, a United States partner, and 98 percent of both book and taxable income was allocated to partners who were Dutch banks – foreign partners who were not liable for United States taxes and thus were indifferent to the U.S. tax consequences of their participation in the partnership. The allocations were technically correct under the allocation rules of § 704(b) and the regulations thereunder. (See Chapter 4, Section 2.) The partnership had very large book depreciation deductions and no tax depreciation. As a result, most of the partnership's taxable operating income, which was substantially in excess of book taxable income, was allocated to the tax-indifferent foreign partners, even though a large portion of the cash receipts reflected in that income was devoted to repaying the principal of loans secured by property that GECC had contributed to the partnership. The overall partnership transaction saved GECC approximately $62 million in income taxes. The District Court allowed the claimed deductions finding nothing in the applicable regulations to prevent the shifting of taxable income to the tax indifferent partner. The District Court judge indicated that even though one of the principal motivations for the transaction was to avoid taxes, the transaction was economically real. TIFD-III-E, Inc. v. United States, 342 F.Supp.2d 94 (D.Conn. 2004). Reversing the District Court, the Court of Appeals held, under the facts and circumstances test of Commissioner v. Culbertson (text page 12), that the Dutch Bank's interest was in the nature of the debt interest of a secured lender, "which would neither be harmed by poor performance of the partnership nor significantly enhanced by extraordinary profits." The Second Circuit's analysis followed the approach of other Circuit Courts, which avoided detailed analysis of the transaction under the economic substance doctrine in favor of findings that the Dutch Banks in other versions of this transaction were not partners. *Boca Investerings Partnership v. United States*, 314 F.3d 625 (D.C. Cir. 2003), rev'g 167 F. Supp. 2d 298 (D.D.C. 2001), *cert denied*, 540 U.S. 826 (2003); *Saba Partnership v. Commissioner*, 273 F.3d 1135 (Fed. Cir. 2001); *ASA Investerings Partnership v. Commissioner*, 201 F.3d 505 (D.C. Cir. 2000), *cert. denied*, 531 U.S. 871 (2000); *ACM Partnership v. Commissioner*, 157 F.3d 231 (3d Cir. 1998), *cert. denied*, 526 U.S. 1017 (1999);

Notwithstanding the Second Circuit's strong opinion that the arrangement in the *Castle Harbour* case did not constitute a partnership, on remand, 660 F. Supp. 2d. 367 (D. Conn. 2009), the district court again held the arrangement to be a partnership, this time by applying § 704(e), discussed in the text at pages 180-183. It would not be surprising if the district court's decision is again reversed on appeal.

Although § 704(e) is headed 'Family Partnerships," § 704(e)(1) itself makes no reference to family partnerships. It provides as follows.

A person shall be recognized as a partner for purposes of this subtitle if he owns a capital interest in a partnership in which capital is a material income-producing factor, whether or not such interest was derived by purchase or gift from any other person.

In *Evans v. Commissioner*, 447 F.2d 547 (7th Cir. 1971), aff'g 54 T.C. 40 (1970), the court held that the application of § 704(e)(1) was not limited to the context of family partnerships, where an interest in a partnership frequently is acquired by gift rather than by purchase, but is applicable whenever capital is a material income producing factor in a partnership. Evans was a somewhat unusual case. The taxpayer, who was a partner in a general partnership in which capital was a material income producing factor, assigned his partnership interest (and not merely the right to income) to his wholly owned corporation. The taxpayer never told his partner of the assignment — indeed he denied it had occurred — and after the assignment under state law the taxpayer remained a partner viz-a-vis the other partner and third parties. Nevertheless, the court concluded that despite these facts and notwithstanding the *Culberson* principle, § 704(e)(1) compelled the conclusion that for federal income tax purposes the taxpayer was no longer a partner, but that his wholly owned corporation was the partner. Therefore, the taxpayer was not subject to tax on the income attributable to the interest assigned or upon the gain realized upon a subsequent sale of the partnership interest to the other partner. The most critical factor to the court's conclusion was that under the relevant state law the corporation, as the assignee of the taxpayer's partnership interest, was entitled to receive the profits to which the assigning partner would otherwise be entitled, and on dissolution of the partnership the assignee was entitled to receive the assignor's interest. Thus, the corporation having the right to income and a distributive share of assets, obtained for federal income tax purposes a capital interest in the partnership.

Although *Evans* applied § 704(e)(1) to determine who, between two different persons, was the partner, in the family context § 704(e) frequently is applied to determine whether a partnership exists in the first place. Until *Castle Harbour*, however, § 704(e)(1) never was applied to determine whether an arrangement between business entities or unrelated individuals was partnership. *Castle Harbour* is unique in applying § 704(e)(1) to determine whether a partnership existed between different business entities.

## B. PARTNERSHIP VERSUS CORPORATION

**Page 31:**

**In the first line of the final paragraph change** "Treas. Reg. § 301.7704-1(b)" to "Treas. Reg. § 1.7704-1(b)."

**Page 32:**

**In the sixth line of the carryover paragraph, change** "Treas. Reg. § 301.7704-(d)" to "Treas. Reg. § 1.7704-(d)."

**In the last line of the first full paragraph, change** "Treas. Reg. § 301.7704-(h)" to "Treas. Reg. § 1.7704-(h)."

**In the fourth line of the second full paragraph, change** "Treas. Reg. § 301.7704-(j)" to "Treas. Reg. § 1.7704-(j)."

# CHAPTER 2

# FORMATION OF THE PARTNERSHIP

## SECTION 1. CONTRIBUTION OF MONEY OR PROPERTY

**Page 40:**

**After the carryover paragraph insert:**

Prop. Reg. § 1.108-8 (2008) would provide that the fair market value of a partnership interest received by the creditor in exchange for debt is the liquidation value of the interest under properly maintained partnership capital accounts if the partnership treats the liquidation value of partnership interest as its fair market value. This valuation rule would apply only if the debt for equity exchange is an arm's-length transaction and subsequent to the exchange the creditor's partnership interest is not redeemed by either the partnership or a person related to the partnership in a transaction that is intended to avoid cancellation of indebtedness income by the partnership. If these requirements are not satisfied, then the value of a partnership interest received in exchange for debt would be determined based on all of the facts and circumstances.

Prop. Reg. § 1.721-1(d) (2008) would provide that § 721 would apply to the creditor's contribution of debt to the partnership in exchange for a partnership interest. Thus, the creditor would not recognize gain or loss on the exchange of partnership debt for a partnership interest. The creditor's basis in the partnership interest would be determined under § 722. However, under the proposed regulation the nonrecognition rule of § 721 would not apply to a transfer of a partnership interest in satisfaction of a partnership indebtedness for unpaid rent, royalties, or interest.

**Page 43:**

**In the twenty-second line of the first paragraph, change** "§ 709(b)(2)" **to** "§ 709(b)(3)."

---

## SECTION 2. CONTRIBUTION OF ENCUMBERED PROPERTY

**Page 47:**

**In the tenth line of the second full paragraph, change** "Treas. Reg. § 1.752-(g), Ex." **to** "Treas. Reg. § 1.752-(g), Ex. (1)."

**SECTION 3. CONTRIBUTION OF PROPERTY VERSUS CONTRIBUTION OF SERVICES**

### A. TREATMENT OF THE PARTNER RECEIVING A PARTNERSHIP INTEREST IN EXCHANGE FOR SERVICES

**Page 52:**

**Replace the second sentence of the second full paragraph with the following:**

If the partner makes a § 83(b) election, any increase in the value of the partnership interest between the date the service partner is admitted to the partnership will not be taxed as compensation when the restriction lapses, but instead will be converted into capital gain realized at a later time.

### B. TREATMENT OF THE PARTNERSHIP ISSUING A PARTNERSHIP INTEREST IN EXCHANGE FOR SERVICES

**Page 69:**

**In the second line after the block quote in the first full paragraph, change** "Treas. Reg. § 1.1031-1(a)" **to** "Treas. Reg. § 1.1031-2(a)."

# CHAPTER 3

# TAXATION OF PARTNERSHIP TAXABLE INCOME TO THE PARTNERS

## SECTION 1.    PASS-THRU OF PARTNERSHIP INCOME AND LOSS

**Page 83:**
**At the end of the first full paragraph of the *ILLUSTRATIVE MATERIAL*, insert:**

Thus, in Burke v. Commissioner, 485 F.3d 171 (1st Cir. 2007), the taxpayer was required to include in income the taxpayer's distributive share of partnership income even though partnership assets were held in an escrow account agreed to by the partners pending resolution of a dispute between the two law firm partners on how to divide the proceeds of their law partnership.

**Page 86:**

**Replace the last sentence of the first full paragraph with the following:**

The resolution of this issue affects whether expenses may be deducted currently or must be capitalized and amortized over 180 months under § 195.

**After the second full paragraph, insert:**

Although a partner is generally treated as engaged in the trade or business of a partnership in which the partner is a member, Rev. Rul. 2008-12, 2008-10 I.R.B. 520, concludes that a limited partner in a partnership engaged in the trade or business of trading securities is subject to the investment interest limitation of § 163(d) on the partner's distributive share of the partnership's interest deduction. Section 163(d)(5)(A)(ii) provides that the term "property held for investment" includes any interest held by a taxpayer in an activity involving the conduct of a trade or business that is not a passive activity and with respect to which the taxpayer does not materially participate. Temp. Reg. § 1.469-1T(e)(6) provides that trading personal property for the account of owners of an interest in the activity (without regard to whether or not the activity is a trade or business) is not a passive activity. Thus, the distributive share of partnership interest of a partner who is not a material participant is investment interest described in § 163(d)(3). As such it is subject to the § 163(d) limitation on the deduction of investment interest. Rev. Rul. 2008-38, 2008-31 I.R.B. 129, adds that investment interest allocated to a partner in a partnership engaged in the trade or business of trading securities is, nonetheless, deductible above the line in calculating adjusted gross income.

**Page 91:**

**In the note to the table at the top of the page, change** "Temp. Reg. § 1.706-1(b)(3)" **to** " Treas. Reg. § 1.706-1(b)(3)."

# CHAPTER 4

# DETERMINING PARTNERS' DISTRIBUTIVE SHARES

## SECTION 2.    THE SECTION 704(b) REGULATIONS

### A. ALLOCATIONS OF ITEMS UNRELATED TO NONRECOURSE DEBT

### (1) ECONOMIC EFFECT

**Page 127:**

**Delete the table in the middle of the page and insert:**

| | Assets | | | Liabilities and Partners' Capital Accounts | | |
|---|---|---|---|---|---|---|
| | Book | Tax Basis | | | Book | Tax Basis |
| Property | $60,000 | $60,000 | Debt | | $140,000 | |
| | | | C | | ($ 70,000) | $70,000 |
| | | | D | | ($ 10,000) | 0 |
| | $60,000 | $60,000 | | | $60,000 | $70,000 |

(Note that the $10,000 disparity between the partnership's inside basis and the sum of the partners' outside bases is caused by $10,000 gain recognized by D on the distribution in excess of basis for which there is no basis adjustment. I.R.C. § 731(a)(1).)

**Delete the table at the bottom of the page and insert:**

| | Assets | | | Liabilities and Partners' Capital Accounts | | |
|---|---|---|---|---|---|---|
| | Book | Tax Basis | | | Book | Tax Basis |
| Property | $30,000 | $30,000 | Debt | | $140,000 | |
| | | | C | | ($110,000) | $30,000 |
| | | | D | | 0 | $10,000 |
| | $30,000 | $30,000 | | | $30,000 | $40,000 |

**Page 129:**

**Delete the first full paragraph and insert:**

Treas. Reg. § 1.704–1(b)(3) provides rules governing the determination of a partner's interest in a partnership that must be used if the partnership agreement does not allocate partners' distributive shares or if the allocation in the agreement does not have substantial economic effect. Under the regulation, all of the facts and circumstances are to be taken into account. The regulation states that except for allocations of deductions attributable to nonrecourse debt, the allocation with respect to any particular item of partnership income, gain, deduction, loss, or credit does not necessarily have to correspond to any other partnership item. Factors to be considered include the partners' relative capital contributions, their interests in economic profits or losses (in contrast to tax profits and losses), their interests in cash flow, and the relative rights of the partners upon liquidation. No specific guidance regarding the application of these factors is provided, but Treas. Reg. § 1.704–1(b)(5), Ex. (1)(i) and (ii), (4)(i), (5)(i) and (ii), (6), (7), and (8) illustrate reallocation of items according to the partners' interests in a partnership. In PNRC Limited Partnership v. Commissioner, T.C. Memo. 1993–335, the Tax Court held that the allocation of losses in the partnership agreement did not have substantial economic effect because the limited partner was not required to restore a negative capital account. Taking into account the specific facts, losses were allocated in proportion to capital contributions, which was most consistent with the partners' interests in the partnership.

## (2) SUBSTANTIALITY

**Page 138:**

**After the last full paragraph, insert:**

Treas. Reg. § 1.704-1(b)(2)(iii)(d) provides that in determining the substantiality of an allocation to a look-through entity that is a partner, the effect of the interaction of the allocation with the tax attributes of the owner of the look-through entity must be taken into account. Look-through entities include a partnership, S corporation, estate, trust, disregarded entity, and controlled foreign corporation that owns at least 10 percent of the capital or profits of the partnership. In addition, in the case of an allocation to a corporate partner that is a member of a consolidated group, the effect of the allocation on the tax attributes of members of the group is taken into account.

(3) "BUSINESS PURPOSE AND "TAX AVOIDANCE" WITH RESPECT TO PARTICULAR ALLOCATIONS

**Pages 144-145:**

**Delete the material beginning at the top of the page, through the first full paragraph on page 145, and insert:**

Nonetheless, the Commissioner's argument in *Gershkowitz* that the allocation should be disregarded because it had a tax avoidance purpose and the court's recitation that the purpose of the 1976 amendment to § 704(b) was to permit partnerships to use special allocations for bona fide business purposes, but not for tax avoidance purposes, raises the question of whether an allocation which meets the mechanical tests of the regulations may be invalidated if it has a tax avoidance purpose. In TIFD-III-E, Inc. v. United States, 342 F.Supp.2d 94 (D.Conn. 2004), *rev'd* 459 F.3d 220 (2d Cir. 2006), discussed in this supplement at page 2, the District Court concluded that satisfaction of the mechanical rules of the regulations under § 704(b) transcends both an intent to avoid tax and the avoidance of significant tax through agreed upon partnership allocations. The Second Circuit reversed finding that the arrangement did not create a partnership.

The District Court's opinion in the *Castle Harbour* case generated significant commentary suggesting that the court erred in its determination that the allocations had substantial economic effect. See, e.g., Karen C. Burke, Castle Harbour: Economic Effect and the Overall-Tax-Effect Test, 107 Tax Notes 1163 (May 30, 2005). Although the allocations might have had economic effect under Treas. Reg. §1.704–1(b)(2)(ii), the allocations were not substantial under Treas. Reg. §1.704–1(b)(2)(iii). The factual analysis is quite complex. Because the income stream was completely predictable and under the partnership agreement the end result was that the Dutch banks merely recouped their investment plus a guaranteed 8.5 percent return, the allocations were not substantial under Treas. Reg. §1.704–1(b)(2)(iii)(*a*) because as a result of the allocations, when compared to an allocation of book income that simply reflected the amounts actually to be ultimately distributed to the partners under the agreement, the after-tax economic consequences of the other partners were enhanced, and there was a strong likelihood that the after-tax consequences to the Dutch banks would not be diminished.

## B. ALLOCATIONS ATTRIBUTABLE TO NONRECOURSE DEBT

**Page 147:**

**Replace the first sentence following the balance sheet at the top of the page with the following:**

Because the amount of the nonrecourse debt encumbering the depreciable asset is $180, and its book value/tax basis is only $160, the partnership has $20 of minimum gain with respect to the asset after year 1, and $20 of the $40 of depreciation in the first year was a nonrecourse deduction.

## SECTION 3. ALLOCATIONS WITH RESPECT TO CONTRIBUTED PROPERTY

**Page 157:**

**At the end of the carryover paragraph, insert:**

Prop. Reg. § 1.704-3(a)(1) (2008) would add that these allocation methods apply only to contributions to a partnership that "are otherwise respected" as contributions of property to a partnership and which are not recast as a different transaction under the anti-abuse rules of Treas. Reg. § 1.701-2.

**Delete the second sentence of the first full paragraph and insert:**

Thus, in the AB Partnership example, if the partnership sold the property for $800, A would be allocated $400 of tax gain and B would be allocated no gain for tax purposes.

**Page 159:**

**Delete the first sentence of the first full paragraph and insert:**

Consider the AB Partnership discussed in the preceding examples, which recognized a $400 tax gain and a $200 book loss on the sale for $800 of property contributed by A.

**Page 162:**

**Replace the table headed "Cross Allocations of § 704(c) Depreciation" with the following.**

## Cross-Allocations of § 704(c) Depreciation

| Asset | Book | Basis | E Book | E Tax | F Book | F Tax |
|---|---|---|---|---|---|---|
| Machinery (contributed by E) 5 years | $1,000 | $ 750 | | | | |
| Machinery Depreciation | $ 200 | $ 150 | $100 | $ 50 | $100 | $100 |
| Equipment (contributed by F) 10 years | $1,000 | $1,500 | | | | |
| Equipment Depreciation | $ 100 | $ 150 | $ 50 | $ 50 | $ 50 | $100 |
| | | | $150 | $100 | $150 | $200 |

**Page 166:**

**Delete the fourth and fifth full sentences on this page of the carryover paragraph and insert:**

The same allocations would be made in each of years 2 through 5. In years 6 through 10, tax depreciation would be zero.

**Page 167:**

**At the end of the second full paragraph insert:**

Treas. Reg. § 1.704-3(a)(10) requires that in testing for a reduction in the partners' aggregate tax liabilities, the impact on indirect owners must be taken into account. Indirect partners include the owners of interests in a pass-through entity that is a partner, including a partnership, an S corporation, an estate or trust, or a controlled foreign corporation that is a 10 percent partner. Furthermore, as amended in 2010, Treas. Reg. § 1.704-3(a)(1) provides that the use of allocation methods with respect to built-in gain or loss property only apply to contributions to a partnership that "are otherwise respected." Even though an allocation may comply with the literal language of Treas. Reg. § 1.704-3(b), (c), or (d) (traditional method, curative allocations, or remedial allocations), "the Commissioner can recast the contribution as appropriate to avoid tax results inconsistent with the intent of subchapter K." Under the regulation, remedial allocations among related parties are one factor that may be considered.

**Page 167:**

**Replace the paragraph under** "3. DE MINIMIS EXCEPTION" **with the following:**

3. DE MINIMIS EXCEPTION

To avoid complexity where the disparity between the book value and basis of contributed property is small, Treas. Reg. § 1.704–3(e)(1) permits a partnership to disregard § 704(c) entirely if the aggregate fair market value of all properties contributed by a partner does not differ from their aggregate adjusted bases by more than 15 percent of basis *and* the total disparity for all properties contributed by the partner during the year does not exceed $20,000. If the de minimis rule is satisfied, alternatively, the partnership may elect to allocate gain or loss upon disposition, but not depreciation, under § 704(c). In applying the basis - book disparity test, built-in gains and losses are both treated as positive numbers. Thus, for example, if A contributes cash to the AB Partnership and B contributes Blackacre, with a basis of $1,000 and a fair market value of $19,000, and Whiteacre, with a basis of $5,000 and a fair market value of $4,000, the de minimis rule applies because the aggregate disparity between basis and book value is $19,000 (($19,000 − $1,000) + ($5,000 − 4,000)). But if Whiteacre were worth only $2,000, the disparity between basis and book value would be $21,000 (($19,000 − $1,000) + ($5,000 − 2,000)), and the de minimis rule would not apply. Note that the de minimis rule applies partner-by-partner. Thus for example, if A contributed Blackacre, with a basis of $1,000 and a fair market value of $19,000, and B contributed Whiteacre, with a basis of $5,000 and a fair market value of $4,000, the de minimis rule would not apply to either property applies because the aggregate disparity between basis and book value with respect to the property contributed by each partner exceeds 25 percent of the property's basis. Thus, the de minimis test exception rarely applies

**Page 170:**

**After the first full paragraph, insert:**

A management or investment partnership is permitted by Treas. Reg. § 1.704-3(e)(3) to aggregate built-in gains and losses from qualified financial assets, rather than follow the normal property-by-property approach required by regulations For purposes of making reverse allocations of recognized gains and losses under § 704(c) principles, Rev. Proc. 2007-59, 2007-40 I.R.B. 745, provides automatic permission to aggregate built-in gains and losses to a qualified partnership, which is a partnership that allocates gains and losses in proportion to the partners' capital accounts, which reasonably expects to revalue its assets at least four times a year, which holds publicly traded property of at least 90 percent of its non-cash assets, has at least 10 unrelated partners, and will make at least 200 trades of financial assets during the year.

## SECTION 5. ALLOCATIONS WHERE INTERESTS VARY DURING THE YEAR

**Pages 174-175:**

**Replace the last full paragraph on page 174 and the first full paragraph on page 175 with the following:**

Treas. Reg. § 1.706–1(c)(2), issued under the pre–1976 version of § 706, prescribes two methods for taking into account the partners' varying interests during the year when a partner sells his entire interest or retires; the interim closing of the books method and the proration method.. These regulations do not specifically address the method to be used on admission of a new partner by contribution or on a disposition of less than all of a partner's interest. However, the legislative history of pre–1984 § 706(c)(2)(B), the 1976 statutory predecessor to § 706(d)(1), indicates that the same methods are to be used, S.Rep. No. 94–938, 94th Cong., 2d Sess. 97–98 (1976), and judicial application of pre–1984 § 706(c)(2)(B) employed these methods. See Richardson v. Commissioner, 76 T.C. 512 (1981), aff'd, 693 F.2d 1189 (5th Cir.1982).

Regulations proposed twenty-five years after the 1984 adoption of the current § 706(d)(1), would mandate the interim closing of the books method, whenever a partner's interest is changed, including a partner's retirement or sale of the partner's entire interest in the partnership, unless the partnership by agreement among the partners elects to use the proration method. Prop. Reg. § 1.706-4(a)(1) (2009). For purposes of determining allocations to partners whose interests vary during the taxable year, the proposed regulations would require the partnership to allocate partnership items under its method of accounting for the full taxable year to segments of the taxable year representing discrete periods during which partners' interests vary. Prop. Reg. § 1.706-4(a)(2) (2009).

Under the interim closing of the books method, Prop. Reg. § 1.704-4(c)(2) (2009) would allow the partnership to allocate items to a segment of the taxable year ending either on the calendar day a partner's interest changes, or adopt a semi-monthly convention under which a change in a partner's interest during the first fifteen days of a month would require the partnership to close its books as of the last day of the preceding month, and a change in a partner's interest after the fifteenth day of the month would require the partnership to close its books on the fifteenth day of the month of the change. Prop. Reg. § 1.706-4(e) (2009). Under the proration method, the partnership's items for the entire year would be prorated over the full taxable year and allocated among the partners based on their respective percentage interests during each segment of the taxable year. Prop. Reg. § 1. 706-4(d)(1) (2009). A segment would end on the calendar day on which a partner's interest changes. Prop. Reg. § 1.706-4(d)(2) &(e)(1) (2009).

Prop. Reg. § 1.706-4(d)(3) (2009) contains special rules under the proration method that would prevent a prorated allocation of "extraordinary" items, which is a problem under the current regulations for a partner who disposes of the partner's entire interest by liquidation or sale. The proposed regulations would require an allocation of extraordinary items that, in general, arise on a disposition of partnership property to the partners in proportion to their interests at the beginning of the calendar day on which the extraordinary item is taken into account. Extraordinary items include, among others, gain or loss on the disposition or abandonment of capital assets, trade or business property, property excluded from capital gains treatment under § 1221(a)(1), (3), (4), or (5) if substantially all of the assets in a particular category are disposed of in one transaction, discharge of indebtedness, and items from the settlement of tort or third-party liability.

The proposed regulations are not entirely clear whether the presence of extraordinary items precludes use of the proration method for the partnership's regular operating income and related items. The direction to account for extraordinary items is contained in the proposed regulations' description of the use of the proration method, which seems to suggest that the allocation of extraordinary items to a calendar day is an exception to the proration of other items. However, Prop. Reg. § 1.706-1(a)(1) (2009) requires that, "The partnership and all of its partners shall use the same method (interim closing or proration) . . . for all variations in the partners' interests occurring within each partnership taxable year." This language suggests that if an extraordinary item must be accounted for on the calendar day on which the item is incurred, all items must be accounted for under the same method. On the other hand, the treatment of extraordinary items is described as part of the proration method, and the accounting treatment for extraordinary methods may have been intended by the drafters of the proposed regulations as a permissible variation within that method. Hopefully the IRS will clarify this issue before the regulations are finalized..

**Page 176:**

**At the end of the first full paragraph, insert:**

But see Prop. Reg. 1.706-4(d)(3) (2009), which would require allocation of certain extraordinary items, such as gain or loss on the disposition of partnership assets, among the partners in proportion to their partnership interests on the day an extraordinary item is accounted for.

**Page 178:**

**After the first full paragraph, insert:**

Prop. Reg. § 1.706-4(b) (2009) would expressly provide that the rules for allocating items to partners whose interest varies will not apply to changes in the allocation of the distributive share of partnership items as long as the variation in partnership interests is not attributable to a contribution of money or property to the partnership and the allocations resulting from a modification satisfy the partnership allocation rules of § 704(b). In addition, the proposed regulations would allow service partnerships to adopt any reasonable method to account for varying interests of the partners during a taxable year in which allocations are valid under § 704(b).

# CHAPTER 5

# ALLOCATION OF PARTNERSHIP LIBILITIES

## SECTION 1. ALLOCATION OF RECOURSE LIABILITES

**Page 188:**

**Delete the last sentence of the carryover paragraph and insert:**

Thus, for example, the risk on a nonrecourse loan to a partnership from a corporation in which a partner owns more than eighty percent of the stock is treated as borne entirely by the shareholder-partner.

**Page 190:**

**Replace the last sentence of the first full paragraph with the following:**

Treas. Reg. § 1.752–2(k) provides that in determining the extent to which a partner bears the economic risk of loss for a partnership liability under Treas. Reg. § 1.752–2, payment obligations of a disregarded entity are taken into account only to the extent of the net value of the disregarded entity's assets (including the disregarded entity's enforceable rights to contributions from its owner, but excluding the disregarded entity's interest in the partnership and the fair market value of property pledged to secure a partnership liability, minus the disregarded entity's liabilities), except to the extent the owner of the disregarded entity is otherwise required to make a payment with respect to the disregarded entity's obligation.

# Chapter 6

# Transactions Between Partners and the Partnership

## Section 1. Transactions Involving Services, Rents and Loans

**Page 217:**

**After the last full paragraph, insert:**

In Wallis v. Commissioner, T.C. Memo. 2009-243, the taxpayer (a tax lawyer) retired as a partner in his law firm and, among other amounts, received $240,000 in twelve $20,000 payments over four taxable years. The $240,000 represented accumulated amounts that had been awarded to him as an equity partner over many years, but which were neither currently distributable in the years they were awarded nor recorded in the partner's capital account. Rather, the amounts, which were determined annually without regard to partnership income, were payable over a period of time after the partner reached age 68, but were forfeitable if the partner left the firm before that date. The Tax Court held that the payments were a guaranteed payment under § 707(c) and § 736(a), taxable as ordinary income, and were not received as distributions under § 731.

**Page 220:**

**Delete the second full paragraph and insert:**

Jenkins v. Commissioner, 102 T.C. 550 (1994), suggested that a § 707(c) payment to a partner retiring due to disability might be excludable under former § 104(a)(3), but did not resolve the issue; the court merely held that it had jurisdiction to decide whether former § 104(a)(3) excluded the payment.

**Page 229:**

**After the last paragraph, insert:**

Rev. Rul. 2007-40, 2007-25 I.R.B. 1426, held that the transfer of appreciated property by a partnership to a partner in satisfaction of a guaranteed payment owed to the partner is a sale or exchange of the property by the partnership and not a distribution under § 731. Thus the partnership is required to recognize gain on the transfer. The ruling does not deal with whether the partnership is entitled to deduct the value of the property or whether it must capitalize that amount, as the case may be.

# CHAPTER 7

# SPECIAL LIMITATIONS ON LOSS DEDUCTIONS AT THE PARTNER LEVEL

## SECTION 1. THE AT RISK RULES OF SECTION 465

**Page 256:**

**After the first full paragraph, insert:**

In Hubert Enterprises v. Commissioner, T.C. Memo 2008-46, the taxpayer owned 99 percent of the units of a limited liability company taxed as a partnership that purchased equipment financed with debt that was recourse to the LLC, but which was not guaranteed by any LLC member. The LLC agreement required members to restore a deficit capital account on liquidation of the LLC in order to pay creditors and to satisfy the positive balance of another member's capital account. Applying the ultimate liability standard of Emershaw v. Commissioner, text, page 256, because the case was appealable to the Sixth Circuit, the Tax Court held that the taxpayer had no personal liability, because repayment of any deficit was contingent on liquidation of the LLC and no creditor had a right to force a liquidation under state law. Thus, the taxpayer was not at-risk with respect to the LLC's recourse debt, which could not be enforced directly against the partner.

## SECTION 3. THE PASSIVE ACTIVITY RULES OF SECTION 469

**Page 264:**

**After the last paragraph, insert:**

Garnett v. Commissioner, 132 T.C. No. 19 (2009), held that an interest in a limited liability company (or a limited liability partnership) is not treated as a limited partnership interest under § 469(h)(2). Thompson v. United States, 87 Fed. Cl. 728 (2009) reached the same result. Both courts reasoned that § 469(h)(2) treats limited partners differently because of an assumption that limited partners do not materially participate in their limited partnerships. In an LLC, on the other hand, all members have limited liability but members may participate in management. Thus, whether or not the taxpayer is a material participant requires a full factual inquiry in which a taxpayer can demonstrate material participation in the activity by using any of the seven tests in Temp. Reg. § 1.469-5T(a) . The IRS has acquiesced in Garnett and Thompson AOD 2010-02 (March 9, 2010)

**Page 266:**

**After the third full paragraph, insert:**

Treas. Reg. § 1.469-2(f)(6) contains a special rule providing that rental income from property that is rented for use in a trade or business in which the taxpayer is a material participant is treated as active income. In Beecher v. Commissioner, 481 F.3d 717 (9th Cir. 2007), the taxpayers rented office space to two corporations in which the taxpayers were material participants. The taxpayers also had other rental properties that produced net passive activity losses. Upholding the validity of the self-rental rule in Treas. Reg. § 1.469-2(f)(6), the court held that the taxpayers' rental income from leases to the taxpayers' active businesses was active income and could not be reduced by the taxpayer's passive activity loss from other rental activities. Accord Krukowski v. Commissioner, 279 F.3d 547 (7th Cir. 2002); Sidell v. Commissioner, 225 F.3d 103 (1st Cir. 2000), and Fransen v. United States, 191 F.3d 599 (5th Cir. 1999).

# CHAPTER 8

# SALES OF PARTNERSHIP INTERESTS BY THE PARTNERS

## SECTION 1. THE SELLER'S SIDE OF THE TRANSACTION

### A. GENERAL PRINCIPLES

**Page 271:**

**In the citations the Internal Revenue Code, change** "1(h)(6)(B), (7)(A)" **to** "1(h)(5)(B), (6)(A)."

**Page 276:**

**After the carryover paragraph, insert:**

In Kornman Associates v. United States, 527 F.3d 443 (5th Cir. 2008), the court held that an obligation to replace property sold in a short sale represented a liability for purposes of § 752. In a notorious abusive tax shelter transaction, taxpayers would enter into a short sale of some commodity (currency or Treasury notes) then contribute the proceeds of the short sale and the obligation to acquire the property sold to a partnership. In *Kornman*, the taxpayer sold short Treasury notes and contributed the $102.5 million proceeds and the obligation to replace the Treasury notes to a partnership in exchange for a 99 percent partnership interest. Subsequently the taxpayer sold the partnership interest for a $1.8 million promissory note from the purchaser and claimed a capital loss based on a $102.5 million basis in the partnership interest. The Fifth Circuit held that the taxpayer's obligation to replace the Treasury notes was a liability includible in amount realized on disposition of the interest. See Treas. Reg. § 1.752-1(a)(4)(ii). Cemco Investors, LLC v. United States 515 F.3d 749 (7th Cir. 2008), reached the same result on substantially the same facts.

### B. CAPITAL GAIN VERSUS ORDINARY INCOME: SECTION 751

**Page 294:**

**In the third line of the last paragraph, change** "§ 1(h)(7)" **to** "§ 1(h)(6)."

In the sixth line of the last paragraph, change "§ 1(h)(7)(A)" to "§ 1(h)(6)(A)."

**Page 295:**

In the first line of the first full paragraph, change "§ 1(h)(6)(B)" to "§ 1(h)(5)(B)."

---

## SECTION 2. THE PURCHASER'S SIDE OF THE TRANSACTION

**Page 296:**

**In the citations to the Internal Revenue Code, change** "743" to "743(a)-(d).

**In the citations to the Regulations, change** "1.197-2(h)(12)(iv)(A)" to "1.197-2(g)(3), (h)(12)(v).

**In the citations to the Regulations, add** "Section 1.752-1(d)."

**Page 304:**

**After the formula, insert:**

The amount subtracted under part (2) of this formula will be zero unless the limitation of Treas. Reg. § 1.755-1(b)(2)(i)(B) applies to restrict the amount allocated to capital gains property.

**Page 305:**

**Delete the first sentence after the first fully indented paragraph.**

# CHAPTER 9

# PARTNERSHIP DISTRIBUTIONS

---

## SECTION 1. CURRENT DISTRIBUTIONS

## B. PROPERTY DISTRIBUTIONS

**Page 319:**

**In the citations to the Regulations, add** "Section 1.752-1(d)."

**Page 326:**

**After the first full paragraph, insert:**

Note, however, that Treas. Reg. § 1.752-1(d) treats a liability as assumed by the distributee partner only if (1) the partner is personally obligated to pay the liability, (2) the creditor knows of the assumption and can directly enforce the partner's obligation for the liability, and (3) no other partner (or person that is related to another partner) bears the economic risk of loss for the liability.

---

## SECTION 2. DISTRIBUTIONS IN LIQUIDATION OF A PARTNERSHIP INTEREST

## A. SECTION 736(b) PAYMENTS: DISTRIBUTIONS

**Page 346:**

**After the last paragraph, insert:**

## 2A. DISGUISED CASH DISTRIBUTIONS

In Countryside Limited Partnership v. Commissioner, T.C. Memo. 2008-3, the court rejected the IRS's argument that a distribution of non-tradable, non-marketable corporate notes in liquidation of partners' interests was in effect a distribution of cash resulting in recognized gain in the year of the distribution. The limited partnership held appreciated real property that it intended to sell. Partly through two disregarded LLCs, the partnership borrowed cash which it used to purchase privately issued notes from AIG Matched Funding Corp. In the same year, the partnership distributed the notes to two partners in complete liquidation of their partnership interests, thereby increasing the interests of the remaining general partner and one limited partner. The liquidated partners' bases in their partnership interests were sufficient to offset their shares of partnership liabilities, and the partners claimed that no gain was recognized under § 731(a) on the distribution of the notes as property. The following year the partnership sold its appreciated real property.[5A] Immediately after the sale, the partnership repaid the debt incurred to purchase the notes. Thereafter, the AIG notes held by the liquidated partners were paid. Asserting that the transaction lacked economic substance and violated the anti-abuse rule of Treas. Reg. §1.702-2(a) (text at page 33), the IRS argued that the distribution of the notes was equivalent to a cash distribution that required recognition of gain. The Tax Court was satisfied that, although the transaction was structured to avoid tax, in economic substance the transaction represented a conversion of the taxpayers' investment in the partnership to an investment in 10-year promissory notes, "two economically distinct forms of investment." The court also rejected the IRS's argument that the notes constituted marketable securities under § 731(c)(2)(B)(ii).

---

[5A] The partnership also claimed a basis increase under § 732(b) which reduced the gain recognized on sale of its appreciated real estate. The IRS has challenged the basis increase in an action involving a different partnership year.

**Page 349:**

**After the second paragraph, insert:**

## 5. DISTINGUISHING A LIQUIDATING DISTRIBUTION FROM A CURRENT DISTRIBUTION

7050 Ltd. v. Commissioner, T.C. Memo. 2008-112, suggests that a liquidating distribution cannot occur in steps that straddle two taxable years. One of the issues in case was whether a distribution of property (foreign currency) from the partnership (which was an LLC) was a liquidating distribution, resulting in an exchanged basis for the property determined with reference to the partnership interest pursuant to § 732(b) or a current distribution, resulting in a transferred basis from the partnership pursuant to § 732(a). In 2001, the partnership distributed almost all of its assets (Canadian currency) to its two partners and filed a Cancellation of Domestic Certificate of Limited Partnership with the secretary of state's office in the state in which it had been formed. However, the partnership retained a balance of Can $6,892.16 in its bank account, which was not completely closed until 2003. The partnership also filed 2001 tax return that it labeled "final return." The Tax Court held that the partnership had not liquidated in 2001 and that the distribution was not a liquidating distribution, but rather was a current distribution, with the resulting transferred basis to the partners. For a partnership to terminate "section 708(b)(1)(A) *** require[s] complete cessation of all partnership activity, including the distribution to the partners of all the partnership's assets. *** Holding Canadian currency in a bank account is quite similar to the kinds of minimal activity that we've already found were enough to keep a partnership unterminated." The partnership was not terminated, and the partners did not receive liquidating distributions, until the partnership's bank account. Accordingly, the partners took a transferred basis in the Canadian currency under § 732(a), not an exchanged basis under § 732(b).

## SECTION 3. BASIS ADJUSTMENTS TO REMAINING PARTNERS

**Page 363:**

**Delete the first full paragraph.**

**Pages 363-364:**

**Delete the last sentence beginning on page 363 and carrying over to page 364.**

## SECTION 4. SALE OF INTEREST TO OTHER PARTNERS VERSUS DISTRIBUTION

**Pages 378-381:**

**Delete the material in "2. PROPOSED DISGUISED SALE REGULATIONS" and insert:**

Regulations proposed in 2004 would have applied principles similar to the disguised sales rules of Treas. Reg. §§ 1.707-3 through 1.707-6 to treat a distribution to a partner as a disguised sale of a partnership interest. Prop. Reg. § 1.707-7 (2004). The proposed regulations would have adopted a facts and circumstances inquiry based on ten non-exclusive factors. Prop. Reg. § 1.707-7(b)(2). The proposed regulations also would have provided a presumption that transfers to and from a partnership within two years would be treated as a sale, and transfers to and from a partnership more than two years apart would not be treated as a sale. The proposed regulations were withdrawn in 2009 after the Treasury Department and the IRS received written comments, presumably highly critical. Ann. 2009-4, 2009-8 I.R.B. 597. The Announcement indicates that the "Treasury Department and the IRS will continue to study this area and may issue guidance in the future. Until new guidance is issued, any determination of whether a transfer between a partner or partners and a partnership is a transfer of a partnership interest will be based on the statutory language, guidance provided in legislative history, and case law."

## SECTION 7. PARTNERSHIP MERGERS AND DIVISIONS

**Page 408.**

**At the end of the first full paragraph, insert:**

Prop. Regs. §§ 1.704-4(c)(4)(2007) and 1.737-2(b)(2007) would adopt the approach of Rev. Rul. 2004-43. Under the proposed regulations, following an assets-over partnership merger, the seven year holding period of §§ 704(c)(1)(B) and 737(b) with respect to built-in gain property contributed to the merged partnership would begin on the date of the original contribution of built-in gain property to the merged partnership. However, the seven year period would recommence with respect to built-in gain present in property transferred from the merged partnership to the continuing partnership at the time of the merger, reduced by the amount of original built-in gain at the time of contribution. The IRS reserved consideration of the treatment of built-in losses.

# PART II

# TAXATION OF CORPORATIONS AND SHAREHOLDERS

## CHAPTER 10

## TAXATION OF CORPORATE INCOME

### SECTION 1. THE REGULAR CORPORATE INCOME TAX

**Page 419:**

**At the end of the first full paragraph, insert:**

See Rainbow Tax Service, Inc. v. Commissioner, 128 T.C. 42 (2007) (because tax return preparation and bookkeeping services constitute accounting services under § 448(d)(2)(A) and Temp. Reg. § 1.448-1T(e)(5)(vii), Ex. 1(i), the taxpayer employee-owned-corporation was subject to the 35% flat-rate corporate tax under §11(b)(2)). In Grutman-Mazler Engineering Inc v. Commissioner, T.C. Memo. 2008-140, the taxpayer corporation had two shareholders, a 60 percent shareholder was a licensed engineer who performed engineering services for the corporation and oversaw its activities, and a forty percent shareholder who had an engineering degree, but was not a licensed civil engineer, and worked in a "planning division." In determining whether the taxpayer corporation was a "qualified personal service corporation" as defined under § 448(d)(2), the court held that state law is relevant to determine whether an activity is within a qualifying field. Under the relevant state law (California) civil engineering includes submitting designs, plans, tentative tract maps, grading plans, and engineering reports to local governments and coordinating other professionals. thus was performing "engineering service." Therefore, because both shareholders performed services that constituted "engineering" under California law and the other conditions of § 448 were met, the corporation's income was taxed under § 11(b)(2), not at graduated rates.

# CHAPTER 12

# FORMATION OF THE CORPORATION

## SECTION 1. RECEIPT OF STOCK FOR PROPERTY

### A. BASIC PRINCIPLES

**Page 487:**

**At the end of the second full paragraph, insert:**

Prop. Reg. § 1.358-1(g)(1) (2009) would provide that the as long as none of the property transferred to the corporation is itself corporate stock, the aggregate basis of the stock received, i.e., the aggregate basis of the property transferred, as adjusted for any gain recognized, must be allocated among all of the shares of stock received in proportion to the fair market values of each share of stock

Adopting the tracing principles of Treas. Reg. § 1.358-2 applicable to stock for stock exchanges in corporate reorganizations, text page 1028, Prop. Reg. § 1.358-2(g)(2) (2009) would provide that in the case of a § 351 exchange in which stock is transferred to the corporation, and no liabilities are assumed, the basis of each share of stock received in the exchange will be the same as the basis of the share or shares transferred in exchange. Under this rule, if shares representing different blocks of stock are transferred to the corporation in exchange for more than one share, the basis of the different blocks of stock will be reflected in the bases of the stock received for each block. If more than one share is received in exchange for a share transferred, then the basis of the transferred share would be apportioned to the shares received by the fair market value of the shares received. Treas. Reg. § 1.358-2(a)(2)(i), Prop. Reg. 1.358-2(b)(2) (2009). If fewer shares are received than the number of shares transferred, the allocation of the basis of the transferred shares would be made in some manner that reflects the fact that each share received was acquired on the same date and with the same basis as the shares transferred. Treas. Reg. § 1.358-2(a)(2)(i), Prop. Reg. § 1.358-2(b)(3) (2009).

### C. "SOLELY FOR STOCK"—THE RECEIPT OF OTHER PROPERTY

**Page 499:**

**After the heading *ILLUSTRATIVE MATERIAL,* insert:**

A1. ALLOCATING BOOT.

Prop. Reg. § 1.351-2(b) (2009) would promulgate the holding of Rev. Rul. 68-55 in regulations. The proposed regulation would provide that in determining the amount of gain recognized in a § 351 transaction the fair market value of each category of consideration received is allocated to the transferred properties in proportion to the relative fair market value of each of the transferred properties.

---

## SECTION 2. "SOLELY" FOR STOCK: ASSUMPTION OF LIABILITIES

A. BASIC PRINCIPLES

**Page 506:**

**Delete the third full sentence of the carryover paragraph.**

B. LIABILITIES IN EXCESS OF BASIS

**Page 523:**

**In the table at the bottom of the page, in the Blackacre column, change the number for** "Gain (loss) realized" **from $550 to $450.**

**Page 529:**

**In the second full paragraph, fourth line, replace the citation to § 451(h) with a citation to § 461(h).**

**Page 530:**

**After the carryover paragraph, insert:**

The Federal Claims Court in *Coltec Industries* was reversed by the Federal Circuit. Coltec Industries, Inc. v. United States, 454 F.3d 1340 (Fed. Cir. 2006). The Circuit Court of Appeals agreed that there was nothing in §§ 358(d) and 357(c)(3) that required Garlock to reduce its basis in the stock by the amount of the liabilities assumed by the controlled corporation, Garrision. However, the Circuit Court held that the lower court erred by failing to apply the economic substance doctrine in order to recognize that the transaction had no meaningful purpose except for the tax benefits. The Court thus held that the transactions should be disregarded for tax purposes.

**Page 531:**

**In the second sentence of the carryover paragraph, replace** "Temp. Reg. § 1.358-5T" **with** "Treas. Reg. § 1.358-5".

## SECTION 3. THE CONTROL REQUIREMENT

**Page 533:**

**Replace the last sentence of the carryover paragraph with the following:**

(The taxpayer apparently took the position that the public, which together with the associates held over 80 percent of the combined voting power, was not a transferor of property, and the Tax Court did not consider the possibility that the public collectively might be viewed as a transferor of property to the corporation along with the associates.)

# CHAPTER 13

# THE CAPITAL STRUCTURE OF THE CORPORATION

## SECTION 1.    DEBT VERSUS EQUITY

**Page 564:**

**After the first full paragraph, insert:**

The Sixth Circuit's opinion in Indmar Products Co., Inc. v. Commissioner, 444 F.3d 771 (6th Cir. 2006), illustrates the weighing of multiple factors to classify shareholder advances to a closely held corporation as debt. Indmar was 100 percent owned by the members of a single family. Various family members advanced funds to Indmar, although not in proportion to their stockholdings. Initially the shareholder advances were not represented by written notes, but that was changed in 1993. Notes reflecting the advances provided for payment on demand and a 10 percent interest rate, which was higher than the rate paid by the company for its commercial bank financing. The Court indicated that the notes were structured as demand loans to give the creditors flexibility to demand payment to meet their needs. However, the notes were classified as long term debt under Tennessee State law, which required an agreement that the note holders would forego payment for twelve months. The note holders regularly demanded and received payment of both interest and principal. The corporation had not paid any dividends. Interest and principal payments were made when requested by shareholder-note holders. The Tax Court, T.C. Memo 2005-32, held that the notes were equity interests and denied Indmar's interest deductions for payments to the note holders. The Sixth Circuit reversed. Stressing that no factor is controlling, the Court listed the factors it developed in Roth Steel Tube Co. v. Commissioner, 800 F.2d 625, 629-630 (6th Cir. 1986), including (1) the names given to the instruments, if any, evidencing the indebtedness; (2) the presence or absence of a fixed maturity date and schedule of payments; (3) the presence or absence of a fixed rate of interest and interest payments; (4) the source of repayments; (5) the adequacy or inadequacy of capitalization; (6) the identity of interest between the creditor and the stockholder; (7) the security, if any, for the advances; (8) the corporation's ability to obtain financing from outside lending institutions; (9) the extent to which the advances were subordinated to the claims of outside creditors; (10) the extent to which the advances were used to acquire capital assets; and (11) the presence or absence of a sinking fund to provide repayments. With respect to the nature of the notes as demand notes without fixed dates for payment of interest and principal, the court observed that, "Where advances are documented by demand notes with a fixed rate of interest and regular interest payments, the lack of a maturity date and schedule of payments does not strongly favor equity. To give any significant weight to this factor would create a virtual per se rule against the use of demand notes by stockholders, even though '[m]uch commercial debt is evidenced by demand notes.'" The Sixth Circuit also discounted Indmar's failure to pay dividends, which is not listed as a factor in its *Roth Steel* decision. Ultimately the Sixth Circuit concluded that eight of the eleven *Roth Steel* factors favored debt status, two of the factors, the absence of fixed maturity dates and the absence of a sinking fund deserved little weight under the facts before the Court, and the absence of security for the note did not outweigh the other factors.

**Page 570:**

**After the first full paragraph, insert:**

Hubert Enterprises, Inc. v. Commissioner, 230 Fed. Appx. 526 (6th Cir. 2007) involved a similar but slightly different transaction. The taxpayer, a closely held family corporation, advanced $2.4 million to a limited liability company (a tax partnership) owned by family members. The loan was represented by a demand note with no fixed maturity date, was not secured, and called for interest payable at the applicable federal rate. The borrower made only one payment of interest on the note. The court denied the taxpayer's claimed bad debt deduction under § 166 for the worthless note, finding that the note was equity under the factors specified in the Sixth Circuit's opinion in Roth Steel Tube Co. v. Commissioner, 800 F.2d 625 (6th Cir. 1986), discussed at page 31 of this supplement. Further, the Sixth Circuit also affirmed the Tax Court holding that the corporation was not entitled to deduct the amount advanced to the LLC as a loss of capital because the corporation had no ownership interest in the LLC. The advance represented a constructive dividend conferring an economic benefit on its shareholders (the owners of the LLC).

# CHAPTER 14

# DIVIDEND DISTRIBUTIONS

## SECTION 2. DIVIDEND DISTRIBUTIONS IN GENERAL

**Page 617:**

**At the end of the first full paragraph, insert:**

Prop. Reg. § 1.301-2 (2009) would adopt the rule of *Johnson* to provide that the portion of a distribution that is not a dividend will be applied to reduce the basis of each share within the class of stock on which the distribution is made pro rata on a share-by-share basis. As a consequence, the distribution may reduce require recognition of gain under § 301(c)(3) with respect to some shares while the distributee shareholder retains basis in other shares.

**Page 618:**

**At the end of the fourth full paragraph, insert:**

See Rev. Rul. 2009-25, 2009-38 I.R.B. 365 (interest paid by a corporation on a loan to purchase a life insurance policy on an individual for which a deduction has been disallowed under § 264(a)(4) reduces earnings and profits for the taxable year in which the interest would have been allowable as a deduction but for its disallowance under § 264(a)(4)).

## SECTION 4. DISGUISED DIVIDENDS

**Page 644:**

**After the carryover paragraph, insert:**

In Beckley v. Commissioner, 130 T.C. No. 18 (2008), the taxpayer's wife made a loan to a corporation in which the taxpayer was a shareholder to develop a working model of Web-based video conferencing software. The corporation had financial problems and the working model was transferred to a new corporation in which the taxpayer was a shareholder. The new corporation made payments to the taxpayer's wife, a portion of which was reported as taxable interest income and the balance of which was treated as a repayment of the principal she lent to the first corporation. The IRS accepted the taxpayer's wife's reporting, but treated a portion of the payments received by the taxpayer's wife as constructive dividends to the taxpayer. The IRS asserted that because there was no written loan agreement, under the state statute of frauds the corporation was not liable for the debt and that payments to the taxpayer's wife were made to satisfy only the taxpayer's personal obligations. The Tax Court concluded that "the existence of an oral agreement . . . may cause [a state] court to enforce an oral agreement if unjust enrichment would occur if the oral agreement were not enforced," and, in any event, the corporation's "conduct in actually making payments . . . establish the loan repayment character of the payments and the principal and interest nature thereof." Accordingly, the court found that payments on the loan did not constitute a constructive dividend to the taxpayer.

**Page 647:**

**After the second full paragraph, insert:**

Cox Enterprises Inc. v. Commissioner, T.C. Memo. 2009-134, demonstrates that not all transactions that result in a diminution of corporate assets necessarily result in constructive dividend treatment, but the case is very unusual and probably does not provide support for avoiding constructive dividend treatment except on substantially similar facts. In that case, a corporation that was a member of the Cox Enterprises affiliated group of corporations, transferred the assets of a television station to a partnership in exchange for a majority interest in the partnership in a transaction that normally would be tax-free under § 721. Two family partnerships, the partners of which were family members of three trusts that together held a 98 percent majority interest in the Cox Enterprises parent corporation, contributed cash to the partnership and received minority interests. The IRS asserted that under § 311(b), the Cox Enterprises corporate group recognized gain on the transfer to the trusts of a portion of the partnership interest it received in exchange for the assets because the partnership interest received by the Cox Enterprises group member that transferred the assets was worth $60.5 million less than the value of the transferred assets. The IRS's theory was that the Cox Enterprises group had constructively distributed as a dividend an economic portion of its partnership interest to the shareholder trusts by transferring to family partnerships "for the benefit of" the shareholder trusts. On the taxpayer's motion for summary judgment, for purposes of the motion, the $60.5 million disparity was between the value of the assets and the value of the partnership interest it received in return was admitted. The Tax Court found that the undisputed facts established that Cox Enterprises' primary purpose was not to provide an economic benefit to the family partnerships and, derivatively, to the shareholder trusts. In summarizing the applicable case law, the court quoted *Gilbert v. Commissioner*, 74 T.C. 60, 64 (1980): "'[T]ransfers between related corporations can result in constructive dividends to their common shareholder if they were made primarily for his benefit and if he received a direct or tangible benefit.' If the benefit to the shareholder is 'indirect or derivative in nature, there is no constructive dividend.'" Applying this legal standard to the factual conclusion, there was not a constructive dividend to the shareholder trusts, even though an economic benefit was conferred on the beneficiaries of the shareholder trusts. Accordingly, no gain was recognized under § 311(b). The court rejected the IRS's argument that to find a constructive dividend "it is only necessary to establish that appreciated assets left the corporate solution …, for the benefit of its Shareholder Trusts, to establish that there has been a distribution with respect to [the] Shareholder Trusts' stock to which section 311 applies."

## SECTION 5.     INTERCORPORATE DIVIDENDS

**Page 652:**

**After the carryover paragraph, insert:**

In OBH, Inc. v. United States, 397 F.Supp.2d 1148 (D. Neb. 2005), the court refused to apply § 246A to reduce OBH's (formerly known as Berkshire Hathaway) § 243 dividend received deduction with respect to dividends received on its portfolio stock investments, because the court found that OBH's indebtedness was not directly traceable to its acquisition of dividend-paying stock. Although an Internal Revenue Service agent testified that he was able to trace loan proceeds to stock purchases, the court concluded that there was no direct or immediate connection between the funds that OBH borrowed and the stock it purchased, and that the agent's findings were based on arbitrary allocations of funds among numerous transactions over a period of several months. The court's conclusion was reinforced by its acceptance as credible of Warren Buffet's uncontradicted testimony that the dominant purpose in incurring the indebtedness was to increase and fortify the corporation's capital base, and that at the time the taxpayer engaged in the borrowing transactions, Buffett, who personally made the investment decisions, did not know how the debt proceeds would be invested.

# CHAPTER 15

# STOCK REDEMPTIONS

## SECTION 1. INTRODUCTION

**Page 660:**

**In the twenty-third line of the first full paragraph of the *ILLUSTRATIVE MATERIAL*, change** "§ 312(f)" **to** "§ 312(n)(7)."

**Page 661:**

**In the tenth line of the first full paragraph, change** "all ten of C's shares," **to** "all ten of A's shares".

**In the fourth line from the bottom of the first full paragraph, change the formula** "($30/3) ÷ (6 × 30/360)" **to** "($30/3) × (6 × 30/360)".

## SECTION 2. SUBSTANTIALLY DISPROPORTIONATE REDEMPTIONS

**Page 668:**

**After the carryover paragraph, insert:**

In H.J. Heinz Co. v. United States, 76 Fed. Cl. 570 (2007), the taxpayer attempted to take advantage of the shift in basis of redeemed stock to other stock in order to generate a capital loss. Heinz Credit Company (HCC, a Delaware lending subsidiary formed to minimize state taxes on intercompany loans) purchased on the open market 3,500,000 shares of its parent's [H.J. Heinz] stock with cash acquired from commercial lenders. H.J. Heinz redeemed 3,325,000 of these shares giving HHC a subordinated zero coupon convertible note. H.J. Heinz and HHC treated the transaction as a dividend from H.J. Heinz to HCC under §§ 301 and 302(d). HCC thus asserted that its basis in the full 3,500,000 shares shifted to its remaining 175,000 H.J. Heinz shares. Thereafter, HHC sold the 175,000 shares to an unrelated party claiming a $124 million capital loss, which was reported on the H.J. Heinz consolidated return. See Chapter 19. At the end of three years, HHC converted the note into H.J. Heinz stock. The court found that HCC possessed the benefits and burdens of ownership of the H.J. Heinz stock and that its transfer of the stock to H.J. Heinz met the definition of a redemption under § 317(b). Nonetheless, the court concluded that the transaction was a sham because the only purpose of the transaction was to produce a capital loss to offset capital gains realized on another transaction, and the transaction had no business purpose. The court also applied the step transaction doctrine to disregard the HCC purchase and redemption of shares.

**Delete the text in paragraph** 4.2 *Proposed Regulations,* **and insert:**

The Treasury Department has proposed replacing the basis adjustment rules in Treas. Reg. § 1.302-2(c), which apply when a redemption is treated as a § 301 distribution, with an entirely different regime. Prop. Reg. § 1.302-5 (2009) would provide that the portion of a redemption distribution that is not treated as a dividend, and thus results in a basis reduction under § 301(c)(2), will be applied to reduce the basis of each share of stock held by the redeemed shareholder in the same class of stock that is redeemed. Prop. Reg. § 1.302-5(a)(1) (2009). The basis reduction would be applied pro rata on a share-by-share basis. As a consequence of this share-by-share approach, gain may be recognized under § 301(c)(3) with respect to some shares while the distributee shareholder holds other shares with unrecovered basis. For example, suppose A owns all 100 shares of the common stock (the only class) of X Corporation. At different times, A acquired 50 shares for $100 (block 1) and 50 shares for $200 (block 2). The corporation, which has no earnings and profits, redeems all of A's block 2 shares for $300. Under §§ 302(d) and 301(c)(2) and (3), the redemption proceeds are treated as a recovery of basis then capital gain to the extent the distribution exceeds basis. The $300 distribution of property is applied on a pro rata, share-by-share basis with respect to each of the shares in the redeemed class owned by A before the redemption so that $150 is distributed with respect to each block of stock. A recognizes a $50 capital gain on block 1 ($150-100) under § 301(c)(3) and has $50 of basis remaining in block 2 ($150-200).

Prop. Reg. § 1.302-5(a)(2) (2009) would provide that after a reduction in basis under § 301(c)(2), the redeemed shareholder is treated as exchanging all of the shareholder's shares (including the redeemed shares) in a nonrecognition corporate recapitalization under § 368(a)(1)(E), discussed in the text at page 1103, for the number of shares retained after the redemption in which the basis of each share of stock received retains the same basis as the original shares deemed transferred. See Prop. Reg. § 1.358-2(b) (2009). This tracing rule preserves the basis of different blocks of shares in the shares remaining after redemption. Thus, in the example of the preceding paragraph, A's 100 shares will be treated as recapitalized with each block retaining its initial basis. A's basis in the 50 recapitalized shares remaining after the redemption determined from the shares deemed exchanged would be zero for 25 shares remaining from block 1 and $50 for 25 shares remaining from block 2.

In the case of redemption of all of the shares of the redeemed shareholder that is treated as a dividend distribution, Prop. Reg. § 1.302-5(a)(3) (2009) would provide that the shareholder's unrecovered basis in the redeemed shares is treated as a loss on the date of the redemption, but recognition of the loss is deferred to a subsequent "inclusion date". The inclusion date is the first date on which the redeemed shareholder would qualify for redemption status under § 302(b)(1), (2), or (3) if the facts on that date had been the facts on the date of the redemption (for example, a date on which a related party reduces an ownership interest), or a date on which all of the stock of the redeeming corporation becomes worthless. Prop. Reg. § 1.302-5(b)(4)(i) (2009). With respect to a corporate shareholder, the inclusion date includes the date on which the redeeming corporation disposes of its assets in a taxable transaction and ceases to exist for tax purposes. Prop. Reg. § 1.302-5(b)(4)(ii) (2009).

## SECTION 3. TERMINATION OF A SHAREHOLDER'S INTEREST

**Page 672:**

**In the second full paragraph, second to the last sentence, after** "Tax Court" **insert** "held."

**Pages 677:**

**In the first line of the last paragraph beginning on the page, change** "Prop. Reg. § 1.302-5 (2002)" **to** "Prop. Reg. 1.302-5 (2009)".

## SECTION 4. DISTRIBUTIONS NOT "ESSENTIALLY EQUIVALENT TO A DIVIDEND"

**Page 685:**

**At the end of the last full paragraph, add:**

However, in Conopco, Inc. v. United States, 100 A.F.T.R.2d 2007-5296 (D. N.J. 2007), the District Court held that periodic redemptions of stock from an Employee Stock Ownership Plan (ESOP) trust, the largest of which reduced the trust's interest from 2.7884 percent to 2.7809 percent, which was a reduction of only 7.5 thousandths of one percent (0.0075%), qualified as a dividend (which permitted a corporate deduction for the distribution to the ESOP under § 404(k)(1)). The court concluded that none of the redemption distributions meaningfully reduced the trust's interest in the corporation.[A1]

---

A1. The court also held that the dividend was not a deductible distribution to the ESOP under § 162(k), which bars a deduction for any expense incurred by a corporation in reacquisition of its stock.  Accord, Ralston Purina Co. v. Commissioner, 131 T.C. No. 4 (2008), and General Mills v. United States, 103 A.F.T.R.2d 2009-589 (8th Cir. 2009).

## SECTION 6.  REDEMPTION THROUGH THE USE OF RELATED CORPORATIONS

**Pages 708 - 709:**

**Replace the paragraph beginning on page708 and ending on page 709 with the following:**

Section 304(a)(1) applies to sales of stock in the brother-sister context only if "one or more persons are in control" of each corporation. "Control" for this purpose is defined in § 304(c)(1) as ownership of 50 percent or more of either combined voting power or value of all classes of stock. See Rev.Rul. 89–57, 1989–1 C.B. 90 (an individual who owned less than 50 percent of the voting stock, but more than 50 percent of the total value of the outstanding stock of a corporation, controlled the corporation).  Control of the corporation the stock of which is sold (the issuer) is measured *before* the sale, while control of the corporation to which the stock is sold (the purchaser) is measured *after* the sale (to take account of the possibility that some of the consideration paid for the issuer's stock might be stock of the purchaser). Treas. Reg. § 1.304–5(b). In measuring 50 percent ownership for testing control, the attribution rules of § 318 apply, but §§ 318(a)(2)(C) and 318(a)(3)(C)—dealing with attribution from and to corporations—are applied by substituting a greater than 5 percent threshold of ownership for the normal greater than 50 percent threshold.  I.R.C. § 304(c)(3)(B). (Moreover, there is no minimum ownership threshold for attribution to or from corporations when testing for dividend equivalency under § 302(b). I.R.C. § 304(b)(1).)  Thus, for example, if A owns 30 percent of X Corporation directly and A also owns 30 percent of Y Corporation, which owns the other 70 percent of X Corporation, A owns an additional 21 percent of X Corporation through Y Corporation (70% x 30%). Thus, A owns 51 percent of X Corporation solely for purposes of applying the control test. If A sold one-half of A'S X Corporation stock to Z Corporation, of which A owned one-half of the stock and thus also controlled, after the sale A continues to own 21 percent of X corporation through Y corporation and 15 percent directly.  A also now owns 7.5 percent of X corporation through Z corporation, for a total ownership of 43.5 percent of X corporation.  Thus, A's ownership of X Corporation was reduced from 51 percent to 43.5 percent.

**Page 712:**

**Replace the text in footnote 2 with the following:**

2. Prop. Reg. § 1.304-2(a)(3) (2009) would treat the deemed redemption that is subject to § 301 as a distribution subject to § 302(d) for all purposes of the tax law. To the extent that the deemed § 301 distribution exceeds earnings and profits, the basis of the common stock deemed issued in a § 351 exchange would be reduced on a share-by-share basis under the rules of Prop. Reg. § 1.302-5(a) (2009), discussed in this supplement at the reference to page 668. Under that provision, any unrecovered basis would result in a loss that is not recognized until the occurrence of an inclusion event, which is an event that would qualify the deemed redemption as an exchange transaction under § 302(a) or the stock of the redeeming corporation becomes worthless.

# PART III

# Elective Passthrough Tax Treatment

## Chapter 18

## S Corporations

### Section 2. Eligibility, Election and Termination

### A. Stockholder Rules

**Page 793:**

**After the third full paragraph, insert:**

The test to identify a common ancestor is applied as of the latest of the date the S corporation election is made, the earliest date a family member acquires stock in the S corporation, or October 22, 2004. I.R.C. § 1361(c)(1)(B)(ii). Treas. Reg. § 1.1361-1(e)(3) provides that the test is applied only on the date specified. Thus, a later acquisition of S corporation stock by a family member more than six generations removed from the common ancestor will not affect S corporation status.

**Page 794:**

**Delete the second sentence of the first full paragraph and insert:**

Similarly, under § 1361(c)(2)(A), a grantor trust may continue as an S corporation shareholder for two years following the death of the grantor.

**Page 796:**

**In the third full paragraph, at the end of the second sentence, insert the following footnote 7A:**

7A.  For tax years beginning after 2006, I.R.C. § 641(c)(2) allows an electing small business trust to deduct interest paid on debt incurred to purchase the S corporation stock against the trust's share of S corporation income, thereby offsetting income that is taxed at the highest individual rate.

**Page 797:**

**After the carryover paragraph, insert:**

If a potential income beneficiary of an ESBT becomes disqualified as an S corporation shareholder, the S corporation election will not be terminated if the trust disposes of all of its S corporation stock within one year of the disqualification.  I.R.C. § 1361(e)(2); Treas. Reg. § 1.1361-1(m)(4)(iii).

**At the end of footnote 8, add:**

Treas. Reg. § 1.1361-1(m)(4)(vi)(B) provides that if a trustee has a discretionary power to make distributions to one or more charitable organizations as a class, the organizations will be counted as only one potential income beneficiary.  Organizations actually receiving a distribution will also be counted as a potential income beneficiary.

**After the first full paragraph, insert:**

*2.4 Individual Retirement Accounts*

Rev. Rul. 92–73, 1992–2 C.B. 224, held that a trust qualified as an individual retirement account is not a permitted Subchapter S corporation shareholder because its income is not currently taxed to the beneficiary.  Taproot Administrative Services, Inc. v. Commissioner, 133 T.C. No. 9, held that a custodial Roth IRA is not an eligible shareholder. [8A]  The court agreed with the IRS's rationale in the ruling that IRAs are not eligible S corporation shareholders because the beneficiary of the IRA is not taxed currently on the trust's share of corporate income, unlike the beneficiary of a custodial account or the grantor of a grantor trust who is subject to tax on the pass-through corporate income.  If a Roth IRA were permitted as a shareholder of an S corporation, the income of the corporation owned by a Roth IRA would never be subject to tax.

8A.  Section 1361(c)(2)(A)(iv) allows a bank whose stock is held by an IRA or Roth IRA to elect S corporation status.

## D. REVOCATION OR TERMINATION OF S CORPORATION STATUS

**Page 806:**

**In the first line of the page, replace the citation to "Rev. Proc. 2003-23" with "Rev. Proc. 2003-43".**

**At the end of the carryover paragraph, add:**

Rev. Proc. 2007-62, 2007-41 I.R.B. 786, provides an additional simplified procedure to request relief from a failure to make a timely S Corporation election that is due to a failure to file the required Form 2553. The simplified method is available if the corporation files the Form 2553 within six-months of the due date of the first return of the corporation (including extensions) and the shareholders have reported the S corporation items consistent with a valid election.

## SECTION 3. EFFECT OF THE SUBCHAPTER S ELECTION BY A CORPORATION WITH NO C CORPORATION HISTORY

### A. PASSTHROUGH OF INCOME AND LOSS

(1) GENERAL PRINCIPLES

**Page 815:**

**At the end of the carryover paragraph, add:**

Treas. Reg. § 1.1366-2(a)(5)(ii) requires that losses incurred during the year of a transfer between spouses or former spouses be prorated on the basis of stock ownership at the beginning of the following taxable year.

**After the first full paragraph, insert:**

In Alpert v. United States, 481 F.3d 404 (6th Cir. 2007), the court required that there be an identifiable event that fixes losses with certainty before an S corporation recognizes discharge of indebtedness income that increases the shareholder's basis. In *Alpert* the receiver's report in a nearly completed bankruptcy case indicated that the corporation had insufficient assets to pay its debts. Nonetheless, the court required that the bankruptcy proceeding be completed to constitute the requisite identifiable event.

**Page 816:**

**After the first full paragraph, insert**

Treas. Reg. § 1.108-7(d) treats any shareholder losses from the current year and prior years that have been suspended under the limitation-on-losses rule of § 1366(d) to be net operating losses that are subject to attribute reduction under § 108(b), if pursuant to § 108(a)(1) (A), (B), or (C) cancellation of indebtedness income realized by the S corporation was not recognized. If the S corporation has more than one shareholder during the taxable year of the debt cancellation, each shareholder's disallowed losses or deductions is a pro rata share of the total losses and deductions allocated to the shareholder under § 1366(a) during the corporation's taxable year.   The deemed NOL allocated to a shareholder consists of a proportionate amount of each item of the shareholder's loss or deduction that was disallowed under § 1366(d)(1) in the year of the debt cancellation.

**Page 819:**

**After the third full paragraph, insert:**

A shareholder contribution to capital excluded from the corporation's gross income under § 118 is not tax-exempt income that provides an increase in basis under §§ 1366(a)(1)(A) and 1367. In Nathel v. Commissioner, 131 T.C. No. 17 (2008) , aff'd, 105 A.F.T.R.2d 2010-2699 (2d Cir. 2010), the taxpayer received loan repayments from an S corporation in excess of his basis in the debt. In an attempt to avoid gain recognition, the taxpayer argued that under Gitlitz v. Commissioner, text page 815, capital contributions are permanently excludable from income and thereby constitute tax exempt income under Treas. Reg. § 1.1366-1(a)(2)(vii), which would first restore basis to the taxpayer's outstanding loans to the corporation under § 1367(b)(2)(B) before increasing basis of the taxpayer's stock. The court concluded that under long standing principles shareholder contributions to capital are added to the shareholder's basis in stock (Treas. Reg. § 1.118-1), that equity contributions and debt are treated differently, and that in any event, contributions to capital are not "income" treated as tax exempt

4.5. *Shareholder Advances*

As discussed in paragraph 4.1 of the *ILLUSTRATIVE MATERIAL*, after stock basis is reduced to zero, an S corporation shareholder may claim losses against the basis of any indebtedness of the S corporation held by the shareholder. Repayment of an indebtedness before the basis is restored will result in gain recognition.   However, open account advances and payments are netted at the close of the taxable year so that only net repayment of open account advances during the year (where basis has not been restored) will result in recognized gain. Treas. Reg. § 1.1367-2(a)(2) limits open account debt for this purpose to advances not represented by a written instrument that do not exceed $10,000. Any advance not evidenced by a written instrument that results in the total running net open account advances exceeding $25,000, and each subsequent advance not evidenced by a written instrument, is treated as a separate indebtedness evidenced by a written instrument, subject to the rules of Treas. Reg. § 1.1367-2(d), rather than as open account indebtedness. Treas. Reg. § 1.1367-2(d)(2). In making this determination, Treas. Reg. § 1.1367-2(d)(2) requires that advances and payments on open account debt be netted continually as they occur. Under the regulations, a shareholder may not offset the repayment of one shareholder advance with the basis of another shareholder advance. Treas. Reg. § 1.1367-2(c)(2). Treas. Reg. § 1.1367-2(c)(2) provides that any net increase in basis is applied first to restore the basis of any indebtedness (including open account indebtedness not exceeding $25,000) repaid during the taxable year to the extent necessary to offset any gain that would be realized on the repayment, then to restore the basis of each outstanding indebtedness in proportion to the amount that the basis of each indebtedness had been reduced by losses allowed under § 1367(b)(2)(A). Treas. Reg. § 1.1367-2(d)(1) provides that adjustments to basis of indebtedness are determined and effective as of the close of the taxable year (except as provided in Treas. Reg. § 1.1367-2(d)(2) for the purpose of determining if advances not evidenced by a written instrument exceed $25,000). Thus, the effect of the net advances and repayments is determined at the close of the year, or earlier if the taxpayer has disposed of the open account debt or the debt is repaid.

The regulations reverse the result of the Tax Court's decision in Brooks v. Commissioner, T.C. Memo 2005-204. Together, the Brooks brothers owned 100 percent of Brooks AG Company, a Subchapter S corporation. The stock basis of each shareholder was zero. In 1997 the Brooks brothers each advanced $500,000 to the company in open account transactions, then claimed losses that reduced their respective bases in the indebtedness to zero. On January 5, 1999, the company repaid each shareholder for the $500,000 advance. On December 31, 1999, each Brooks brother advanced $800,000 to the company on open account, which was sufficient to offset any gain on repayment of the first advance and to allow the Brooks brothers to claim additional losses thereby reducing their basis in the indebtedness to zero. The Brooks brothers repeated the pattern in 2000. The company made an $800,000 repayment to each shareholder on January 3, 2000. On December 29, 2000, the Brooks brothers each advanced $1.1 million to the company, which again offset any gain on the repayment that year and permitted the shareholders to deduct losses from the company to the extent of the remaining basis in the advance. The cycle of advances and repayment thus permitted the Brooks brothers to perpetually defer recognition of gain. The Tax Court endorsed this scheme by treating the Brooks brothers' multiple advances and repayments as a single open account indebtedness. Thus, the shareholders were permitted to net the advances and repayments as of the close of the taxable year and avoid recognition of gain on the repayment that occurred early in each taxable year. Under the proposed regulations, however, open account indebtedness in excess of $10,000 will be treated as a separate indebtedness. Thus, under the proposed regulations, repayment of the Brooks brothers' zero basis advances each January would produce recognized income in the amount of the repayment.

## (2)  EFFECT OF INDIRECT CONTRIBUTIONS ON LIMITATION OF LOSS DEDUCTIONS TO SHAREHOLDER BASIS

**Page 833:**

**At the end of the carryover paragraph, insert:**

Maloof v. Commissioner, 456 F.3d 645 (6th Cir. 2007), denied any basis for a shareholder's guarantee of bank loan to corporation. With respect to another loan to the corporation that the shareholder cosigned, and that he thus "could one day be asked to pay" the court likewise denied any basis "because until that contingency transpired the S corporations remained indebted to the bank, not to Maloof."

**Page 835:**

**After the carryover paragraph, insert:**

Miller v. Commissioner, T.C. Memo 2006-125, upheld an increase in the shareholder's basis in the S Corporation as a result of a back-to-back loan arrangement. The case involved a loan that originally had been made directly to the corporation but was restructured.  Although the corporation did not guarantee the loan to the shareholder, the shareholder collaterally assigned to the third party lender his rights under the security agreement running from the corporation to the shareholder-lender

In Kerzner v. Commissioner, T.C. Memo. 2009-76, the taxpayers, who were equal shareholders of an S corporation and equal partners in a partnership, attempted to avoid the § 1366(d) limitation on passed-through losses from an S corporation by borrowing money from the partnership and then lending the loan proceeds to the S corporation, which in turn paid equivalent amounts of rent back to the partnership. The Tax Court disallowed the pass-through losses, holding that the taxpayers did not acquire any basis in indebtedness from the S corporation from the transactions because they involved a circular flow of funds and there was no real expectation that the shareholders would ever repay the borrowed funds. Thus the taxpayers had not incurred any economic outlay.

## SECTION 4.  QUALIFIED SUBCHAPTER S SUBSIDIARIES

**Page 844:**

**After the first full paragraph, insert:**

1.3. *Termination by Stock Sale*

Section 1362(b)(3)(C)(ii), added in 2007, provides that a sale of stock of a Q Sub that results in termination of the subsidiary's Q Sub election (which automatically occurs unless the purchaser is another S corporation that elects to continue the Q Sub election) will be treated as a sale of the Q Sub's assets in proportion to the percentage of the Q Sub stock that has been sold.  The transaction is then treated as a pro rata transfer of the Q Sub's assets by the selling S corporation and the purchaser of the stock to a newly formed C corporation in a transaction governed by § 351. The legislative history indicates that § 351 will apply to the deemed contribution regardless of the percentage of stock of the subsidiary held by the Subchapter S former Q Sub owner, e.g. meeting the 80 percent control requirement of § 351 is not required.  For example, if a Subchapter S corporation sells 21 percent of the stock of a Q Sub, the S corporation will be treated as selling 21 percent of the subsidiary's assets and then contributing the assets to a new corporation in a transaction to which § 351 applies.

## SECTION 5.  S CORPORATIONS THAT HAVE A C CORPORATION HISTORY

### A.  DISTRIBUTIONS FROM AN S CORPORATION WITH EARNINGS AND PROFITS ACCUMULATED FROM SUBCHAPTER C YEARS

**Page 845:**

**At the end of the carryover paragraph, insert footnote 23A.**

[23A]A Subchapter S corporation formed before 1983 also may have accumulated earnings and profits from pre-1983 S corporation years.  The Small Business Job Protections Act of 1996 eliminated pre-1983 S Corporation earnings and profits for any corporation that was a Subchapter S corporation for its first taxable year beginning after December 31, 1996.  Section 8235 of the Small Business and Work Opportunity Tax Act of 2007 (an uncodified provision) finished the job by providing that any corporation that was not an S corporation for its first taxable year beginning after December 31, 1996, may reduce accumulated earnings and profits by an amount equal to any earnings and profits accumulated in pre-1983 S corporation years.  Thus, if an S corporation that otherwise would have had earnings and profits from a year before 1983 makes a distribution in excess of its accumulated adjustment account, any portion of the excess that would have been a dividend if pre-1983 earnings and profits were included in accumulated earnings and profits will now be treated as a return of basis, and then capital gain to the extent it exceeds the stock basis.

## B. PASSIVE INVESTMENT INCOME OF AN S CORPORATION WITH ACCUMULATED EARNINGS AND PROFITS

**Page 849:**

**In the first paragraph of the *ILLUSTRATIVE MATERIAL,* delete the first sentence and insert:**

For purposes of §§ 1362(d)(3) and 1375, passive investment income is defined as income from royalties, rents, dividends, interest, and annuities.

**Page 850:**

**In the third full paragraph, at the end of the second full sentence, insert:**

(Note that the 2007 Act removed gains from the sale of stocks and securities from the definition of passive investment income.)

## C. BUILT-IN GAIN TAX

**Page 854:**

**After the carryover paragraph, insert:**

The 2009 Act created a special rule in § 1374(d)(7) that shortens the recognition period of § 1374 to seven years with respect to property sold in taxable years beginning in 2009 or 2010.  No tax is imposed on recognized built-in gain if the seventh year of the recognition period preceded 2009 or 2010.  The seven year rule applies separately to property acquired by an S corporation from a subchapter C corporation in a transferred basis transaction  so that recognized built-in gain is not subject to tax after the seventh year beginning with the date of acquisition from the C corporation.  See § 1374(d)(8).

# PART IV

# AFFILIATED CORPORATIONS

## CHAPTER 19

## AFFILIATED CORPORATIONS

### SECTION 2. CONSOLIDATED RETURNS

**Page 870:**

**In the citations to the Regulations, delete "-20(a) - (c)."**

**Pages 881-884:**

**Replace the text in section 3.4** *Basis Adjustment and Loss Suspension Rules,* **with the following:**

In some cases, application of the investment adjustment rules conflicts with the principles of §§ 311 and 336, discussed in the text at pages 623 and 760, because it permits assets that are sold out of the consolidated group to obtain a step up in basis without the payment of a current corporate level tax. Suppose, for example, that S Corporation holds a single asset with a basis of $100 and a fair market value of $300. P Corporation purchases all of the stock of S Corporation for $300, P and S do not make a § 338 election, and P and S Corporations elect to file a consolidated return. S Corporation then sells the asset for $300. S Corporation recognizes a $200 gain, and P Corporation increases its basis in the S Corporation stock from $300 to $500. P Corporation then sells the stock of S Corporation for $300, realizing a $200 loss, which offsets the $200 gain. Absent a limitation on the recognition of this loss, tax on the gain realized from the sale of the assets effectively would be eliminated by P Corporation's loss on the sale of the stock of S. P Corporation's tax loss is artificial; it does not reflect an economic loss. The same problem arises if the asset is a depreciable asset which is consumed in the course of S Corporation's business.

To deal with this issue, Treas. Reg. § 1.1502-36 provides "unified rules for loss on subsidiary stock" transferred by a member of an affiliated group filing a consolidated return.[4A] A transfer of a loss share of stock includes any event in which (1) gain or loss would be recognized (apart from the rules in the proposed regulations), (2) the holder of a share and the subsidiary cease to be members of the same group, (3) a nonmember acquires an outstanding share from a member, or (4) the share is treated as worthless. The purpose of these rules is twofold, to prevent the consolidated return provisions from creating non-economic losses on the sale of subsidiary stock and to prevent members of the affiliated group filing the consolidate return from claiming more than one tax benefit from a single economic loss. Under the regulations, any transfer of a loss share (defined as a share of stock of an affiliate having a basis in excess of fair market value) requires the application in sequence of three basis rules.

First, under Treas. Reg. § 1.1502-36(b), a basis redetermination rule is applied to deal with tax losses attributable to investment adjustment account allocations among different shares of stock under Treas. Reg. § 1.1502-32 that result in disproportionate reflection of gain or loss in shares' basis. Second, if any share is a loss share after application of the basis redetermination rule, a basis reduction rule is applied under Treas. Reg. § 1.1502-36(c) to deal with loss duplication attributable to investment adjustment account adjustments, but this reduction does not exceed the share's "disconformity amount." Third, if any duplicated losses remain after application of the basis reduction rule, under Treas. Reg. § 1.1502-36(d) an attribute reduction rule is applied to the corporation the stock of which was sold to prevent the duplication of a loss recognized on the transfer or preserved in the basis of the stock. If a chain of subsidiaries is transferred (rather than a single subsidiary) the order in which the rules are applied is modified. In this case, basis redetermination rule and basis reduction rule are applied sequentially working down the chain, and the attribute reduction rule is than applied starting with the lowest tier subsidiary and working up the chain.

*The Basis Redetermination Rule.* — Under the basis redetermination rule in Treas. Reg. § 1.1502-36(b), investment adjustments (exclusive of distributions) that were previously applied to members' bases in subsidiary stock are reallocated in a manner that, to the greatest extent possible, first eliminates loss on preferred shares and then eliminates basis disparity on all shares. This rule affects both

---

[4A] These regulations replace the basis adjustment and loss suspension rules in Treas. Reg. §§ 1.337(d)-2 and 1.1502-35 for transactions after September 17, 2008. Treas. Reg. §§ 1.337(d)-2(a)(1), 1.1502-35(a)(2)(iii), (j).

positive and negative adjustments, and thus addresses both noneconomic and duplicated losses.   First, The basis of any loss share is reduced by any positive investment adjustments, but the basis will not be reduced to less than the value of the loss shares.   Second, to the extent of any remaining loss on the transferred shares, negative investment adjustments are removed from shares that are not transferred loss shares and are applied to reduce the loss on transferred loss shares.   Third, the positive adjustments removed from the transferred loss shares are allocated to increase basis of other shares only after the negative adjustments have been reallocated.   Note that this rules does not affect the aggregate basis of the shares, and thus has no impact, and thus does not apply, if all of the shares of a subsidiary are sold or become worthless; it is important only when some, but not all, shares are sold.   A number of special limitations on basis reallocation also must be considered in various specific circumstances.

*The Basis Reduction Rule.* — If, after applying the basis redetermination rule in step one, any transferred share is a loss share (even if the share only became a loss share as a result of the application of the basis redetermination rule), the basis of that share is subject to reduction.   The basis reduction rule in Treas. Reg. § 1.1502-36(c) eliminates noneconomic losses that arise from the operation of the investment adjustment account rules.   Under this rule, the basis of each transferred loss share is reduced (but not below its value) by the lesser of (1) the share's disconformity amount, or (2) the share's net positive adjustment.

The "disconformity amount" with respect to a subsidiary's share is the excess of its basis over the share's allocable portion of the subsidiary's inside tax attributes (determined at the time of the transfer).   Every share within a single class of stock has an identical allocable portion.   Between shares of different classes of stock, allocable portions are determined by taking into account the economic arrangements represented by the terms of the stock.   "Net inside attributes" is the sum of the subsidiary's loss carryovers, deferred deductions, cash, and asset bases, minus the subsidiary's liabilities. The disconformity amount identifies the net amount of unrealized appreciation reflected in the basis of the share.

A share's net positive adjustment is computed as the greater of (1) zero, or (2) the sum of all investment adjustments (excluding distributions) applied to the basis of the transferred loss share, including investment adjustments attributable to prior basis reallocations under the basis reallocation rule.   The net positive adjustment identifies the extent to which a share's basis has been increased by the investment adjustment provisions for items of income, gain, deduction and loss (whether taxable or not) that have been taken into account by the group.   Special rules apply when the subsidiary the stock of which is transferred itself holds stock of lower-tier subsidiary.

*The Attribute Reduction Rule.* — If any transferred share remains a loss share after application of the basis reallocation and basis reduction rules, any loss recognized with respect to the transferred share is allowed. However, in this instance, the subsidiary's tax attributes (including the consolidated attributes, e.g., loss carryovers, attributable to the subsidiary) are reduced pursuant to Treas. Reg. § 1.1502-36(d). The attribute reduction rule addresses the duplication of loss by members of consolidated groups, and is designed to prevent the group from recognizing more than one tax loss with respect to a single economic loss, regardless of whether the group disposes of the subsidiary stock before or after the subsidiary recognizes the loss with respect to its assets or operations.

Under the attribute reduction rule, the subsidiary's attributes are reduced by the "attribute reduction amount," which equals the lesser of (1) the net stock loss, or (2) the aggregate inside loss. The "attribute reduction amount" reflects the total amount of unrecognized loss that is reflected in both the basis of the subsidiary stock and the subsidiary's attributes. "Net stock loss" is the amount by which the sum of the bases (after application of the basis reduction rule) of all of the shares in the subsidiary transferred by members of the group in the same transaction exceeds the value of those shares. Treas. Reg. § 1.1502-36(d)(3)(ii). The subsidiary's "aggregate inside loss" is the excess of its net inside attributes over the value of all of the shares in the subsidiary. (Net inside attributes generally has the same meaning as in the basis reduction rule, subject to special rules for lower-tier subsidiaries.) Treas. Reg. § 1.1502-36(d)(3)(iii).

The attribute reduction amount is first applied to reduce or eliminate items that represent actual realized losses, such as operating loss carryovers (Category A), capital loss carryovers (Category B), and deferred deductions (Category C) in that order unless the taxpayer elects to make a different allocation. If the subsidiary does not hold stock of any lower tier subsidiaries, any excess attribute reduction amount is then applied to reduce the basis of assets (Category D) in the asset classes specified in Reg. § 1.338-6(b) other than Class I (cash and general deposit accounts, other than certificates of deposit held in depository institutions), but in the reverse order from the order specified in that section. Thus, the basis in any purchased goodwill is the first item reduced. If the subsidiary holds stock of one or more lower-tier subsidiaries, the Category D attribute reduction is first allocated between the subsidiary's basis in any stock of lower-tier subsidiaries and the subsidiary's other assets (treating the non-stock Category D assets as one asset) in proportion to the subsidiary's basis in the stock of each lower-tier subsidiary and its basis in the Category D assets other than subsidiary stock. Only the portion of the attribute reduction amount not allocated to lower-tier subsidiary stock is applied under the reverse residual method. (Additional special rules apply to prevent excessive reduction of attributes when the subsidiary itself holds stock of a lower-tier subsidiary.) Treas. Reg. § 1.1502-36(d)(4)(ii). If the attribute reduction amount exceeds all of the attributes available for reduction, that excess amount generally has no effect. If, however, cash or other liquid assets are held to fund payment of a liability that has not yet been deducted but will be deductible in the future (e.g., a liability the deduction for which is subject to the economic performance rules of § 451(h)), loss could be duplicated later, when the liability is taken into account. To prevent such loss duplication, the excess attribute reduction amount will be held in suspense and applied to prevent the deduction or capitalization of later payments with respect to the liability. Treas. Reg. § 1.1502-36(d)(4)(ii)(C). Additional special rules apply to prevent excessive reduction of attributes when the subsidiary itself holds stock of a lower-tier subsidiary.

Treas. Reg. § 1.1502-36(d)(4) permits taxpayers to make a protective election to reattribute attributes (other than asset basis) and/or to reduce stock basis (and thereby reduce stock loss) in order to avoid attribute reduction. If an election is made and it is ultimately determined that the subsidiary has no attribute reduction amount the election will have no effect (or if the election is made for an amount that exceeds the finally determined attribute reduction amount, the election will have no effect to the extent of that excess). In addition, taxpayers may elect to reduce (or not reduce) stock basis, or to reattribute (or not reattribute) attributes, or some combination thereof, in any amount that does not exceed the subsidiary's attribute reduction amount.

Finally, if the subsidiary ceases to be a member of the consolidated group as a result of the transfer, the common parent of the group can elect to reduce stock basis (thereby reducing an otherwise allowable loss on the sale of the stock), reattribute attributes, or apply some combination of basis reduction and attribute reattribution alter the otherwise required attribute reduction.

*Worthlessness.* — Treas. Reg. § 1.1502-36(d)(7) provides that, if a member treats stock of the subsidiary as worthless under § 165 (taking into account Treas. Reg. § 1.1502-80(c), text page 884) and the subsidiary continues as a member, or if a member recognizes a loss on subsidiary stock and on the following day the subsidiary is not a member and does not have a separate return year following the recognition of the loss, all Category A, Category B, and Category C attributes (i.e., capital loss carryovers, net operating loss carryovers, and deferred deductions) that have not otherwise been eliminated or reattributed, as well any credit carryovers, are eliminated.

**Page 889:**

**Delete the carryover sentence at pages 889- 890 and insert:**

However, while deferred § 311(b) gain always is included in consolidated taxable income, loss is allowed only if the property subsequently is sold to a nonmember; the deferred loss in excess of the transferee's gain is permanently disallowed if the property is distributed to a nonmember shareholder.

**Page 892:**

**After the second full paragraph, insert:**

**5.2.4A.** *Transactions in which a Member Acquires Debt of a Member*

Treas. Reg. § 1.1502-13(g) addresses the treatment of debt obligations between members of the same group, an "intercompany obligation". The regulations apply to three types of transactions: (1) transactions in which an obligation between a group member and a nonmember becomes an intercompany obligation, for example, the purchase by a consolidated group member of another member's debt from a nonmember creditor or the acquisition by a consolidated group member of stock of a nonmember creditor or debtor (inbound transactions); (2) transactions in which an intercompany obligation ceases to be an intercompany obligation, for example, the sale by a creditor member of another member's debt to a nonmember or the deconsolidation of either the debtor or creditor member (outbound transactions); and (3) transactions in which an intercompany obligation is assigned or extinguished within the consolidated group (intragroup transactions). Treas. Reg. § 1.1502-13(g)(3)(i)(B). In each of these circumstances the following sequence of events is deemed to occur immediately before, and independently of, the actual transaction: (1) the debtor is deemed to satisfy the obligation for a cash amount equal to the obligation's fair market value, and (2) the debtor is deemed to immediately reissue the obligation to the original creditor for that same cash amount. The parties are then treated as engaging in the actual transaction but with the new obligation. Treas. Reg. § 1.1502-13(g)(3)(ii). The regulations contain a number of exceptions to the application of the deemed-satisfaction-reissuance model where it is determined that application of the model is not necessary to achieve the purposes of Treas. Reg. τ 1.1502-13(g) or that burdens associated with valuing the obligation or applying the mechanics of the deemed satisfaction-reissuance model outweigh the benefits achieved by its application.

To avoid misuse of the exceptions to the satisfaction-reissuance model, the regulations provide two anti-abuse rules. The material tax benefit rule applies to an intragroup assignment or extinguishment of an obligation if the transaction is undertaken with a view to shifting built-in items among members to achieve a material tax benefit. Treas. Reg. § 1.1502-13(g)(3)(i)(C). The off-market issuance rule applies if an intercompany obligation is issued at a materially off-market interest rate with a view to shifting of built-in items from the obligation to secure a material tax benefit. In such cases, the intercompany obligation will be treated as originally issued for its fair market value, and any difference between the amount loaned and the fair market value of the obligation will be treated as transferred between the creditor member and the debtor member, as appropriate (for example, as a distribution or a contribution to capital). Treas. Reg. § 1.1502-13(g)(4)(iii).

# PART V

# CORPORATE ACQUISITION TECHNIQUES

## CHAPTER 20

## TAXABLE ACQUISITIONS: THE PURCHASE AND SALE OF A CORPORATE BUSINESS

### SECTION 1.    ASSETS SALES AND ACQUSITIONS

**Page 900:**

**After the carryover paragraph, insert:**

In Solomon v. Commissioner, T.C. Memo. 2008-102, the taxpayers argued that the principles of *Martin Ice Cream Co.* and *Norwalk* should apply, but the Tax Court found those cases to be distinguishable on the facts. In *Solomon*, the corporation (Solomon Colors) of which the taxpayers (father and son) were dominant, but not sole, shareholders and key employees sold one of its several lines of business.   In connection with the sale, the taxpayers entered into covenants not to compete.   Provisions in the contracts described payments received by the taxpayers as consideration for their entering into covenants not to compete, but other documents allocating the purchase price and payments among assets described those payments as consideration for the shareholder's ownership interest in the customer list for the line or business that was sold.  The court rejected the taxpayers' argument that, like in *Martin Ice Cream Co.*, the payments were consideration for the sale of goodwill owned by the shareholders. The *Solomon* court found that the value of the Solomon Colors' business was not attributable to the quality of service and customer relationships developed by the shareholders, which distinguished the facts from *Martin Ice Cream Co.* Because the Solomon Colors' business involved processing, manufacturing, and sale of a product, rather than the provision of services, the corporation's success did not depend entirely on the personal goodwill of its shareholder/employees. Furthermore, the fact that the purchaser did not require the shareholder enter into employment or consulting agreements made it unlikely that it was purchasing their personal goodwill. Accordingly, the payments were entirely consideration for the shareholders' covenants not to compete and thus were ordinary income, not capital gain.

## SECTION 2.   STOCK SALES AND ACQUISITIONS

### Page 918:

### After the third full paragraph, insert:

Twenty two years after § 336(e) was enacted, proposed regulations would extend the provision to sales of the stock of a subsidiary corporation to a taxpayer other than a corporation. Prop. Reg.'s §§ 1.336-0 through 1.336-5 (2008) would generally apply the principles of § 338(h)(10), discussed in the text at page 917, to a "qualified stock disposition," which is a disposition of the stock of a controlled subsidiary that meets the requirements of § 1504(a)(2); stock representing 80 percent voting control and 80 percent of value. See the text, page 875. Prop. Reg. § 1.336-1(b)(5) (2008). A disposition would include both a taxable sale and a taxable distribution of stock representing control of a subsidiary corporation under § 1504(a)(2), including a combination of sales and distributions. Prop. Reg. 1.336-1(a)(4) (2008). The § 336(e) election would not be available in the case of a qualified stock purchase of control by a corporate purchaser under § 338(d)(3). Prop. Reg. § 1.336-1(b)(5)(ii).

In the event of a qualified stock distribution, an election under § 336(e) would allow the selling corporation to treat the distributed subsidiary as selling assets to an unrelated purchaser, then repurchasing the assets for cost. Prop. Reg. § 1.336-2(b)(1) (2009). In most cases the subsidiary would be treated as being liquidated into the seller under § 332. Under principles similar to those of Treas. Reg. § 1.338-4, text page 914, the sales price would be determined as the "aggregate asset deemed disposition price" (ADAD), which would reflect the sales price of sold stock and the fair market value of distributed stock. Prop. Reg. § 1.336-3 (2009). The "adjusted grossed up basis" (AGUB) of the assets deemed purchased by the subsidiary, like AUGB under Treas. Reg. § 1.338 -5, page 913 of the text, is the deemed sales price of the subsidiary's assets grossed up to account for nonrecently purchased stock held by a ten percent or greater shareholder. Prop. Reg. §§ 1.336-4, -1(b)(17) (2008).

# CHAPTER 22

# TAX FREE ACQUISITIVE REORGANIZATIONS

## SECTION 2. THE FUNDAMENTAL RULES GOVERNING REORGANIZATIONS

### A. THE BASIC STATUTORY SCHEME

**Pages 962-963:**

**In section 2 beginning on page 962, Prop. Reg. §§ 1.368-1(d), -2(f), and -2(k), discussed in the text have been finalized. T.D. 9361.**

### B. THE CONTINUITY OF SHAREHOLDER INTEREST REQUIREMENT

### (1) QUALITATIVE AND QUANTITATIVE ASPECTS

**Page 963:**

**In the citations to the Regulations, add** "section 1.368-1T(e)(2)."

**Page 972:**

**In the fourth paragraph, first line, change the citation to** "Treas. Reg. § 1.368-1(e)(2)" **to** "Temp. Reg. § 1.368-1T(e)(2)".

**Page 973:**

**Delete the first full paragraph and insert:**

Under Temp. Reg. § 1.368-1T(e)(2)(iii)(A), a contract provides for fixed consideration if it specifies the number of shares of the acquiring corporation, the amount of money, and the other property (identified by value or by description) that is to be exchanged for the stock of the target corporation. With an Orwellian flourish, Temp. Reg. § 1.368-1T(e)(2)(iii)(B)(1) states that "a contract that provides for contingent consideration will be treated as providing for fixed consideration if it would satisfy the requirements of paragraph (e)(2)(iii)(A) of this section without the contingent adjustment provision." Temp. Reg. § 1.368-

1T(e)(2)(iii)(B)(2) adds that contingent consideration will not be fixed consideration if the adjustments prevent the target shareholders from being subject to the economic benefits and burdens of ownership of the acquiring corporation stock as of the last business day before a binding contract. Thus, adjustments that reflect changes in the value of the stock or assets of the acquiring corporation at a later date will prevent the contract from being treated as providing for fixed consideration. The preamble to the temporary regulations suggests that the contingent consideration provision allows adjustments to the consideration that do not decrease the ratio of the value of the shares of the acquiring corporation to the value of money or other property delivered to the target shareholders relative to the ratio of the value of the target stock to the value of the money or other property that would be delivered to the target shareholders if none of the contingent consideration were delivered. T.D. 9316, 72 F.R. 12974 (2007).

Under Temp Reg. § 1.368-1T(e)(2)(iii), if the target corporation's shareholders may elect to receive either stock or money, the contract provides for fixed consideration if the determination of the number of shares of issuing corporation stock to be provided to the target corporation shareholder is based on the value of the issuing corporation stock on the last business day before the first date there is a binding contract. The preamble to the temporary regulations indicates that the Internal Revenue Service and Treasury believe that if shareholders have an election to receive stock of the acquiring corporation at an exchange rate based on the value of the acquiring corporation stock on the date of a binding contract, the target shareholders are at risk for the economic benefits and burdens of ownership of the acquiring corporation stock as of the contract date. Thus, the preamble concludes that it is appropriate to value the stock of the acquiring corporation as of the signing date for purposes of testing continuity of interest. Temp. Reg. § 1.368-1T(e)(2)(v), Ex. (9) provides an example of the application of the shareholder election.

> On January 3 of Year 1, P and T sign a binding contract pursuant to which T will be merged with and into P on June 1 of Year 1. On January 2 of Year 1, the value of the P stock and the T stock is $1 per share. Pursuant to the contract, at the shareholders' election, each share of T will be exchanged for cash of $1, or alternatively, P stock. The contract provides that the determination of the number of shares of P stock to be exchanged for a share of T stock is made using the value of the P stock on the last business day before the first date there is a binding contract (i.e., $1 per share). Accordingly, the contract provides for fixed consideration, and the determination of whether the transaction satisfies the continuity of interest requirement is based on the number of shares of P stock the T shareholders receive in the exchange and by reference to the value of the P stock on January 2 of Year 1.

Temp. Reg. § 1.368-1T(e)(2)(ii)(A) provides that a binding contract is an instrument enforceable under applicable law.  However, the presence of a condition outside of the control of the parties, such as a requirement for regulatory approval, will not prevent an instrument from being treated as a binding contract.  Temp Reg. § 1.368-1T(e)(2)(ii)(C) provides rules pursuant to which a tender offer can be considered to be a binding contract, even though it is not enforceable against the offerees, if certain conditions are met.  The temporary regulations also provide for modifications of a binding contract.  If the contract is modified to change the amount or type of consideration that the target shareholders would receive, the date of the modification becomes a new signing date for purposes of testing for continuity of interest.  Temp. Reg. § 1.368-1T(e)(2)(ii)(B)(1).  However, if in a transaction that provides for adequate continuity of interest, the contract is modified to increase the amount of stock of the acquiring corporation to be delivered to the target shareholders, or to decrease the amount of cash or value of other property, then the modification will not be treated as a modification of the binding contract.  Temp. Reg. § 1.368-1T(e)(2)(ii)(B)(2).  Similarly, in a transaction that does not qualify as a reorganization for failure to meet the continuity of interest requirement, a modification that reduces the number of shares of stock to be received by the target shareholders, or increases the amount of money or value of property, will not be treated as a modification of the binding contract so that the consideration will continue to be valued as of the signing date.  Temp. Reg. § 1.368-1T(e)(2)(ii)(B)(3).

Temp. Reg. § 1.368-1T(e)(2)(iii)(C) provides that stock that is escrowed to secure customary pre-closing covenants and representations and warranties is not treated as contingent consideration, which would render the safe harbor unavailable.  However, escrowed consideration that is forfeited, is not taken into account in determining whether the continuity of interest requirement has been met.  Temp. Reg. § 1.368-1T(e)(2)(iv), Ex. 2.

Pursuant to § 7805(e)(2), Temp. Reg. § 1.368-2T(e)(2) expired on March 19, 2010.  Notice 2010-25, 2010-14 I.R.B. 527, allows taxpayers to rely on Prop. Reg. § 1.368-1(e)(2) (1007), which is identical to Temp. Reg. § 1.368-2T(e)(2), until new regulations are promulgated. However, "the target corporation, the issuing corporation, the controlling corporation of the acquiring corporation if stock thereof is provided as consideration in the transaction, and any direct or indirect transferee of transferred basis property from any of the foregoing, may not apply the provisions of the proposed regulations unless all such taxpayers elect to apply the provisions of such regulations. This requirement will be satisfied if none of the specified parties adopts treatment inconsistent with this election."

**Pages 973-974:**

The proposed regulations described in the paragraph beginning at the bottom of page 973 have been finalized.  T.D. 9434.

## C. THE CONTINUITY OF BUSINESS ENTERPRISE REQUIREMENT

**Pages 989-990:**

**Delete the paragraph beginning on page 989 and carrying over to page 990 and insert:**

Amendments to Treas. Regs. §§ 1.368-1(d), 1.368-2(f)], and 1.368-2(k) in 2007 significantly liberalized the rules regarding permissible post-acquisition restructurings of a controlled group of corporations involving the target corporation after an otherwise qualifying reorganization. In addition to post-acquisition drops of assets to lower-tier subsidiaries, post-acquisition cross chain transfers and distributions by an acquisition subsidiary that is member of the acquiring corporation's group to a corporation that controls the acquiring corporation of either the target corporation's stock (following a § 368(a)(1)(B) or § 368(a)(2)(E) reorganization) or assets (following a § 368(a)(1)(A), § 368(a)(1)(C), or § 368(a)(2)(E) reorganization) subsequent to the acquisition, do not disqualify the acquisition from reorganization treatment, even though there is no statutory provision expressly providing that such distributions do not affect the validity of reorganization treatment, provided that the distribution would not result in the distributing corporation being treated as liquidated for income tax purposes. The regulations thus permit the acquiring corporation to significantly rearrange ownership of the target corporation's assets or stock, as the case may be, among all of the members of its qualified group (based on § 368(c) control) without disqualifying the reorganization. Furthermore, the regulations permit qualified group members to aggregate their direct stock ownership of a corporation, in a manner similar to aggregation under § 1504(a), in determining whether they have the requisite § 368(c) control of such corporation (provided that the issuing corporation has § 368(c) control in at least one other corporation).

## E. TAX RESULTS TO THE PARTIES TO A REORGANIZATION

### (1) SHAREHOLDERS AND SECURITY HOLDERS

**Page 1026:**

**At the end of the carryover paragraph, insert:**

Prop. Reg. § 1.356-1(b) (2009) would restate these rules by referring to Prop. Reg. § 1.354-1(d)(1) (2009) providing that a pro rata portion of property and money received will be treated as received in exchange for each share of stock or security surrendered based on the fair market value of the surrendered stock or security. The proposed regulations would modify the rule of current Treas. Reg. § 1.356-1(b) by providing that the terms of the exchange agreement specifying the other property or money that is received in exchange for a particular share of stock or security surrendered or a particular class of stock or securities surrendered will control the allocation if the terms are economically reasonable, unless the shareholder's exchange has the effect of a distribution of a dividend.   Where the distribution as the effect of a distribution of a dividend, the proposed regulations would respect an economically reasonable allocation among classes of stock, but not permit an allocation among shares within the same class.  The exchange of a class of stock solely for boot will not be treated as an exchange to which §§ 354 or 356 applies, but will be treated as an exchange to which § 302(d) applies (redemption distributions treated as § 301 distributions).   Prop. Reg. § 1.354-1(d)(2) (2009).

**Page 1027:**

**After the carryover paragraph, insert:**

Prop. Reg. § 1.354-1(d)(1) (2009) would provide that whether the receipt of boot has the effect of a dividend is to be determined by taking into account the overall exchange of all stock.   However, in order to maintain the distinction between different classes of stock, for purposes of determining gain, any boot is allocated pro rata among the shares of a class. If the distribution has the effect of a dividend, the proposed regulations would allow the terms of an exchange to provide economically reasonable allocations of consideration among different classes of stock, but not among shares within a class.

**In the second full paragraph, tenth line, add to the citation to Atlas Tool Co. v. Commissioner the following:**

, aff'd, 614 F.2d 860 (3d Cir. 1980) (specifically rejecting the *Davant* approach)

**Page 1028:**

**In the third full paragraph, ninth and tenth lines, change the citation from "** Treas. Reg. § 1.358-2(a)(4), (c), Ex (3) and (4)" **to Treas. Reg. § 1.358-2(a)(2)(i)."**

**Page 1030:**

**After the second full paragraph, insert:**

Regulations proposed in 2009 restate Treas. Reg. § 1.358-2 with revised section numbering and headnotes, but without substantive change. Prop. Reg. §§ 1.358-1, -2 (2009).

## SECTION 3. STOCK FOR STOCK ACQUISITIONS: TYPE (B) REORGANIZATIONS

**Page 1052:**

### At the end of the fifth full paragraph, insert:

In Notice 2009-4, 2009 I.R.B. 251, the IRS indicted that it continues to believe that the survey methodology of Rev. Proc. 81-70 provides proper guidance for determining the basis of shares received in a Type (B) reorganization. The Notice indicates that the IRS will issue an expanded Rev. Proc. 81-70 with safe harbors to determine the basis of shares acquired from various categories of transferring shareholders, including reporting shareholders, registered non-reporting shareholders, and nominees.

## SECTION 4. STOCK FOR ASSETS ACQUISITIONS: TYPE (C) REORGANIZATIONS

**Page 1060:**

### Delete the fourth full paragraph and insert:

Rev. Rul. 2007-8, 2007-1 C.B. 469, provides that § 357(c)(1), discussed in the text at page 509, will not apply to an acquisitive reorganization notwithstanding the fact that the transaction might also qualify as a § 351 transaction. Rev. Rul. 2007-8 declares obsolete Rev. Rul. 76-188, 1976-1 C.B. 99, which involved a transaction in which a parent corporation transferred all its assets to its wholly-owned subsidiary and the subsidiary assumed all of the parent corporation's liabilities. The liabilities assumed exceeded the basis of the assets transferred to the subsidiary. Section 357(c) was held to be applicable, since the transaction was one "described in" § 351 (a provision to which § 357(c) applies). The prior ruling concluded that the fact that it also constituted a (C) reorganization did not prevent the application of § 357(c), and the parent corporation accordingly recognized a gain on the transaction. Rev. Rul. 2007-8 concludes that since the transferor corporation ceases to exist, it cannot be enriched by the assumption of liabilities.

If brother-sister corporations are involved, it is possible for a (C) reorganization to overlap with § 304, text page 701. It is not clear which provision will control.

## SECTION 5.  TRIANGULAR REORGANIZATIONS

**Page 1070:**

**After the first full paragraph of the block quotation, insert:**

Rev. Rul. 2008-25, 2008-21 I.R.B. 986, dealt with the application of the step transaction doctrine where the target corporation was liquidated after a reverse triangular merger that otherwise would have qualified as a tax-free reorganization. In the ruling, all of the stock of T Corporation was owned by individual A. T had $150x of assets and $50x dollars of liabilities. P Corporation was unrelated to A or T Corporation, and was worth over four times the value of T Corporation. P Corporation formed a controlled subsidiary solely to effect the acquisition, and the subsidiary merged into T Corporation. As a result of the merger, P Corporation acquired all of the stock of T Corporation, and A exchanged the T Corporation stock for P Corporation voting stock worth $90x and $10x in cash and. As part of an integrated plan, following the merger, T Corporation was completely liquidated by P Corporation, transferring all of its assets to P, which assumed all of T Corporation's liabilities. P Corporation continued to conduct the business previously conducted by T Corporation. Apart from the liquidation, the reverse triangular merger otherwise would have qualified as a tax free reorganization under § 368(a)(2)(E). Because of the presence of the cash boot, the merger transaction, standing alone, could not qualify as a tax-free reorganization under § 368(a)(1)(B), or (after taking into account T Corporation's debt) under § 368(a)(1)(C), or under § 368(a)(1)(D) because A did not own sufficient stock of  P Corporation after the merger. The ruling reached two conclusions, first, because both the reverse triangular merger and liquidation occurred pursuant to an "integrated plan," the safe harbor in Treas. Reg. § 1.368-2(k) did not apply and the reverse triangular merger did not qualify as a § 368(a)(2)(E) tax-free reorganization, because after the acquisition, T Corporation did not hold substantially all of its properties. The ruling then held that in characterizing the transactions as other than a reorganization, the step transaction doctrine would not apply. Thus, the first step — the reverse triangular merger — was treated as a § 338(d)(3) qualified stock purchase under Treas. Reg. § 1.338-3(d) and Rev. Rul. 90-95, 1990-2 C.B. 67 (text page 913). The liquidation was a § 332 liquidation, with P Corporation taking a transferred basis under § 334(b) in T Corporation's assets, and T Corporation no recognizing gain or loss pursuant to § 337. In this regard, the ruling reasoned "integrating the acquisition of T stock with the liquidation of T, would result in treating the acquisition of T stock as a taxable purchase of T's assets. Such treatment would violate the policy underlying § 338 that a cost basis in acquired assets should not be obtained through the purchase of stock where no § 338 election is made. Accordingly, consistent with the analysis set forth in Rev. Rul. 90-95, the acquisition of the stock of T is treated as a qualified stock purchase by P followed by the liquidation of T into P under § 332." It is interesting that disqualifying the initial transaction from reorganization status and recharacterizing it as a qualified stock purchase followed by a § 332 liquidation did not affect the ultimate tax treatment of either T Corporation or P Corporation. Only individual A, the shareholder of T Corporation, was affected because A was required to recognize all of the gain or loss. This was so even though apart from tax results, individual A has no interest in or reason to be concerned with whether P Corporation continued to operate T Corporation's business in a continuing T Corporation or as a division of P Corporation, and furthermore, individual A has little or no power over whether or not P Corporation liquidates T Corporation. Note that while the ruling describes the events as occurring pursuant to an "integrated plan," the ruling is silent regarding whether individual A had any knowledge or control over the plan, and it also fails to specify which version of the step transaction doctrine it applied.

## SECTION 6. ACQUISITIVE TYPE (D) REORGANIZATIONS

**Page 1088:**

**After the carryover paragraph, insert:**

*1.1. Cash-Only Distribution Regulations*

Treas. Reg. § 1.368-2(*l*), promulgated in 2009, which replaces similar temporary regulations promulgated in 2006, adopts the long standing judicial and administrative position reflected in *Atlas Tool* that a stock distribution is meaningless when the ownership of the target and acquiring corporations is identical. Treas. Reg. § 1.368-2(*l*)(2)(i) provides that the distribution requirement under §§ 368(a)(1)(D) and 354(b)(1)(B) is deemed to have been satisfied despite the fact that no stock and/or securities are actually issued in a transaction otherwise described in § 368(a)(1)(D) if the same person or persons own, directly or indirectly, all of the stock of the transferor and transferee corporations in identical proportions. For purposes of determining identity of ownership, an individual an all members of the individual's family, as described in § 318(a)(2)(C), will be treated as one individual. In addition, the attribution from entity rules of § 318(a)(2) are applied without regard to the 50 percent ownership limitation for attribution from corporations. Treas. Reg. 1.368-(l)(2)(ii). Complete identity of ownership is not required. The temporary regulations disregard a de minimis variation in ownership. Treas. Reg. § 1.368-2(*l*)(3), Ex. (4) illustrates a de minimis variation with a situation in which A, B, and C each own, respectively, 34%, 33%, and 33% of the transferor's stock and A, B, C, and D each own, respectively,

33%, 33%, 33% and 1% of the transferee's stock. In addition, preferred stock described in § 1504(a)(4) (generally non-voting preferred stock with limited participation in growth, see text page 875), is not taken into account in determining ownership. Treas. Reg. 1.368-2(*l*)(2)(ii).

The regulations provide that if no consideration is received, or the value of the consideration received in the transaction is less than the fair market value of the transferor corporation's assets, the transferee corporation is treated as issuing stock with a value equal to the excess of the fair market value of the transferor corporation's assets over the value of the consideration actually received in the transaction. If the value of the consideration received in the transaction is equal to the fair market value of the transferor corporation's assets, the transferee corporation will be deemed to issue a nominal share of stock to the transferor corporation in addition to the actual consideration exchanged for the transferor corporation's assets. The deemed stock is then deemed to be distributed to the shareholders of the transferor corporation and transferred through chains of ownership to the extent necessary to reflect the actual ownership of the transferee and transferor corporations. Treas. Reg. § 1.368-2(*l*)(2)(i)

Finally, the regulations contain an exception to clarify that the no distribution is necessary rule will not apply to cause a related party triangular reorganization that is a type (A), (C), or (G) reorganization to be treated as a type (D) reorganization. Treas. Reg. § 1.368-2(*l*)(2)(iv).

If an all-cash transaction subject to Treas. Reg. § 1.368-2(*l*) occurs between members of an affiliated group filing a consolidated return, the selling member (S) is treated as receiving the deemed share of stock and any additional stock of the buying member (B) under Treas. Reg. § 1.1502-13(f)(3), which it distributes to its shareholder member (M) in liquidation. Immediately after the sale, the B stock (with the exception of the nominal share which is still held by M) received by M is treated as redeemed in a distribution to which § 301 applies. M's basis in the B stock is reduced under Treas. Reg. § 1.1502-32(b)(3)(v), and under Treas. Reg. § 1.302-2(c), any remaining basis attaches to the nominal share.

**Page 1088:**

**In the first full paragraph, fifteenth line, delete the citation to** Rev. Rul. 75-161, **which was declared obsolete by Rev. Rul. 2007-8, 2007-1 C.B. 469.**

# PART VI

# NONACQUISITIVE REORGANIZATIONS

## CHAPTER 24

## CORPORATE DIVISIONS: SPIN-OFFS, SPLIT-OFFS, AND SPLIT-UPS

### SECTION 2. "ACTIVE CONDUCT OF A TRADE OR BUSINESS," "DEVICE," AND OTHER LIMITATIONS

### B. ACTIVE CONDUCT OF A TRADE OR BUSINESS

**Page 1157:**

**At the end of the carryover paragraph, add:**

In Rev. Rul. 2007-42, 2007-28 I.R.B. 44, the IRS held that a distributing corporation which owned a one-third interest in an LLC that was engaged in the active conduct of a trade or business was itself engaged in the active conduct of a trade or business. The ruling reasons that ownership of a one-third interest in the LLC was significant and that the LLC itself performed the requisite management functions constituting an active trade or business. The ruling also held, however, that ownership of a 20 percent interest in an LLC is not sufficient to constitute the distributing corporation as engaged in an active trade or business.

**Page 1163:**

**After the last paragraph, insert:**

For purposes of determining whether the active business requirement of § 355(b)(1) has been met, under the provisions of § 355(b)(3), Prop. Reg. § 1.355-3(b) (2007) would treat all of the members of a separate affiliated group (SAG) as a single corporation. Thus, the subsidiaries of the common parent of a SAG are treated as divisions of the common parent for purposes of determining whether either the distributing or controlled SAG is engaged in a qualified trade or business.

A corporation's SAG is the affiliated group that would be determined under § 1504(a) if the corporation were the common parent (and § 1504(b) did not apply). See text page 874. Thus, the separate affiliated group of the distributing corporation (DSAG) is the affiliated group consisting of the distributing corporation and all of its affiliated corporations. The separate affiliated group of a controlled corporation (CSAG) is determined in a similar manner, but by treating the controlled corporation as the common parent. Accordingly, prior to a distribution, the DSAG includes CSAG members if the ownership requirements are met. Prop. Reg. § 1.355-3(b)(1)(iii) (2007).

The SAG rule is applied for purposes of determining whether a corporation has conducted a trade or business throughout the requisite five-year period preceding the distribution and whether the distributing and controlled corporations are actively conducting a trade or business following distribution. These proposed regulations will affect the application of the active business requirement in a number of respects.

First, if ownership requirements are met, members of the distributing corporation SAG and the controlled corporation SAG will be treated as belonging to a single SAG during the pre-distribution period, which facilitates identifying the appropriate trades or businesses regardless of how the assets are distributed among the SAG members. See Prop. Reg. § 1.355-3(b)(3)(i) (2007).

Second, the SAG rule applies for purposes of determining whether there has been a taxable acquisition of the trade or business within the five years preceding the distribution under § 355(b)(2)(C) or (D). Because, the subsidiaries of the common parent of a SAG are treated as divisions of the common parent, a stock acquisition of a corporation that becomes a member of a SAG is treated as an asset acquisition (which affects the application of § 355(b)(2)(D) regarding acquisition of control of a corporation conducting an active business). Prop. Reg. § 1.355-3(b)(1)(ii) (2007).

Third, Prop. Reg. § 1.355-3(b)(4)(iii) (2007) permits certain taxable acquisitions of the assets of a trade or business by the distributing corporation without violating the restrictions of § 355(b)(2)(C) and (D), which are interpreted as preventing the use of the assets of distributing to acquire a trade or business in lieu of dividend distributions. The proposed regulations disregard a taxable acquisition by the controlled SAG from the distributing SAG, disregard the use of cash to pay off fractional shares, and to a limited extent, disregard taxable acquisitions from members of the same SAG. However, the proposed regulations do not disregard the recognition of gain or loss in transactions between affiliated corporations unless the affiliates are members of the same SAG. (Analogous to current regulations, taxable acquisitions to expand an existing business within a SAG are disregarded. Prop. Reg. § 1.355-3(b)(3)(ii) (2007)).

Fourth, the application of § 355(b)(2)(D)(i) (control acquired by any distributee corporation) is limited to situations designed to avoid the impact of the repeal of the *General Utilities* doctrine. Thus, the proposed regulations allow a taxable acquisition by a distributee corporation of control of distributing in a transaction where the basis of the acquired distributing stock is determined in whole or by reference to the transferor's basis. Prop. Reg. § 1.355-3(b)(4)(iii)(C) (2007).

Fifth, the proposed regulations interpret § 355(b)(2)(C) and (D) to have the common purpose of preventing the direct or indirect acquisition of the trade or business (to be relied on a distribution to which § 355 would otherwise apply) by a corporation in exchange for assets other than its stock. Thus, if (1) a DSAG member or controlled acquires the trade or business solely for distributing stock, (2) distributing acquires control of controlled solely for distributing stock, or (3) controlled acquires the trade or business from distributing solely in exchange for stock of controlled, in a transaction in which no gain or loss was recognized, § 355(b)(2)(C) and (D) are satisfied. However, if the trade or business is acquired in exchange for assets of distributing (other than stock of a corporation in control of distributing used in a reorganization) § 355(b)(2)(C) and (D) are not satisfied. Under this rule, for example, an acquisition by a controlled corporation (while controlled by the distributing corporation) from an unrelated party in exchange for controlled stock have the effect of an indirect acquisition by distributing in exchange for distributing's assets. Such an acquisition violates the purpose of § 355(b)(2)(C), and will be treated as one in which gain or loss is recognized. Prop. Reg. § 1.355-3(b)(4)(ii) (2007).

## SECTION 3. DISTRIBUTION OF "CONTROL" AND CONTINUITY OF INTEREST REQUIREMENTS

**Page 1190:**

**In the third line of the last paragraph, replace** "Rev. Rul. 79-273" **with** Rev. Rul. 70-225."

## SECTION 4. CONSEQUENCES TO PARTIES TO A CORPORATE DIVISION

**Page 1196:**

**After the first full paragraph, insert:**

Temp. Reg. 1.355-2T(g) (2008), provides that stock of a controlled corporation acquired within the five year period preceding a distribution that causes a controlled corporation to become a member of the separate affiliated group of the distributing corporation, see § 355(b)(3) and the proposed regulations thereunder discussed in this supplement under the reference to page 1163, is not treated as property taxable as boot, but is disregarded in determining whether stock of the controlled corporation is acquired within the five year period. This provision applies to stock of a corporation controlled under the rules of § 368(c) (80 percent of voting control and 80 percent of all classes of stock, at the time of the acquisition but not controlled under the definition of § 1504(a)(2) (80 percent of voting stock and value). Temp. Reg. § 1.355-2T(g)(2). Thus, additional stock of a controlled (but unaffiliated) corporation that is acquired within the five year period preceding distribution, the acquisition of which results in the controlled corporation becoming part of the distributing corporation's affiliated group within the meaning of § 1504, is not treated as other property taxable as boot.

## SECTION 5. DIVISIVE DISTRIBUTIONS IN CONNECTION WITH ACQUISITIONS

**Page 1214:**

**After the second full paragraph, insert:**

1.2.1 *Section 336(e) Election*

A distribution subject to either § 355(d)(2), text page 1199 (50% shareholder with disqualified stock), or § 355(e)(2) carries the potential for gain recognition at three levels: gain recognized by the distributing corporation on distribution of the stock of the controlled corporation, gain recognized by the controlled corporation on distribution of appreciated assets, and gain recognized by the shareholders of the controlled corporation. Section 336(e) provides in the case of a sale or distribution of stock representing control under § 1504(a)(2), text page 875 (80% of voting stock and value), the selling or distributing corporation may elect to treat the sale or distribution as a sale of the assets of the distributed corporation rather than a stock sale. Section 336(e) is discussed in this supplement at the entry to page 918. Prop. Reg. § 1.336-2(b) (2008) would provide rules for a § 336(e) election when the distributing corporation distributes stock of the controlled corporation representing control under § 1504(a)(2) (a "qualified stock disposition") and is required to recognize its realized gain under § 355(d)(2) or (e)(2). If a § 336(e) election is made by the distributing corporation, the controlled corporation is deemed to have sold its assets in a taxable transaction to an unrelated person for an aggregate deemed asset disposition price (Prop. Reg. § 1.336-3 (2008), discussed in this supplement at the entry to page 918), which in general reflects the net fair market value of the assets plus liabilities grossed-up to reflect non-recently disposed stock. The controlled corporation is then deemed to have repurchased its assets for an amount equal to the adjusted grossed basis, determined under the rules of Treas. Reg. § 1.338-5, discussed in the text at page 915. Prop. Reg. § 1.336-2(b)(2)(ii) (2008). Because the controlled corporation is not treated as liquidated, the corporate attributes of the controlled corporation are retained. Corporate attributes are adjusted for the consequence of the deemed asset sale and repurchase. Prop. Reg. § 1.336-2(b)(2)(vi) (2008).

The distributing corporation would not recognize gain or loss on the qualified stock disposition of the stock of the controlled corporation. Prop. Reg. § 1.336-2(b)(2)(iii) (2008). The deemed sale and repurchase of assets by the controlled corporation also would not cause the distribution to fail the requirements of § 355. Prop. Reg. § 1.336-2(b))(2)(v) (2008).

# PART VII

# CORPORATE ATTRIBUTES IN REORGANIZATIONS AND OTHER TRANSACTIONS

## C H A P T E R 25

## CARRY OVER AND LIMITATION OF CORPORATE TAX ATTRIBUTES

### SECTION 2. LIMITATIONS ON NET OPERATING LOSS CARRYVOERS FOLLOWING A CHANGE IN CORPORATE OWNERSHIP

**Page 1250:**

**After the first full paragraph, insert:**

Notice 2010-50, 2010-27 I.R.B. 12, provides guidance for measuring owner shifts of loss corporations that have more than one class of stock outstanding when the value of one class of stock fluctuates relative to another class of stock. The IRS will accept use of the "full value methodology," under which all shares are "marked to market" on each testing date. Under this method, the percentage of stock owned by any person is determined with reference to "the relative fair market value of the stock owned by such person to the total fair market value of the outstanding stock of the corporation. ... [C]hanges in percentage ownership as a result of fluctuations in value are taken into account if a testing date occurs, regardless of whether a particular shareholder actively participates or is otherwise party to the transaction that causes the testing date to occur ... ." The IRS also will accept use of the "hold constant principle." Under this methodology, "the value of a share, relative to the value of all other stock of the corporation, is established on the date that share is acquired by a particular shareholder. On subsequent testing dates, the percentage interest represented by that share (the "tested share") is then determined by factoring out fluctuations in the relative values of the loss corporation's share classes that have occurred since the acquisition date of the tested share. Thus, as applied, the hold constant principle is individualized for each acquisition of stock by each shareholder." The "hold constant principle" has several variations that the notice identifies as acceptable. An acquisition is not an event upon which the acquiring shareholder marks to fair market value other shares that it holds under any hold constant principle variation. To be acceptable, whichever methodology is selected must measure the increased percentage ownership represented by a stock acquisition by dividing the fair market value of that stock on the acquisition date by the fair market value of all of the outstanding stock of the loss corporation on that date. Any alternative treatment of an acquisition is inconsistent with § 382($l$)(3)(C) and is not acceptable. Any method selected, whether the full value methodology" or a particular variation of the "hold constant principle" must be applied consistently to all testing dates in a "consistency period." With respect to any testing date, the consistency period includes all prior testing dates, beginning with the latest of: (1) the first date on which the taxpayer had more than one class of stock; (2) the first day following an ownership change; or (3) the date six years before that testing date.

**Page 1262:**

**After the second full paragraph, insert:**

Treas. Reg. § 1.382-7 provides that for the purposes of computing the § 382 limitation, income received before a change date that is attributable to services to be performed after the change date is not treated as recognized built-in gain. This includes income that is received prior to the change date where recognition is deferred under § 455 (pre-paid dues of certain membership clubs), Treas. Reg. § 1.451-5 (advance payments for goods or long-term contracts), or Rev. Proc. 2004-4, 2004-1 C.B. 991 (certain advance payments that are deferred on financial statements).

**Page 1275:**

**After the first full paragraph, insert:**

10. ECONOMIC STIMULUS EXCEPTION

Section 382(n), enacted as part of the American Recovery and Reinvestment Act of 2009, provides that the § 382 limitation will not apply to an ownership change that results from a restructuring required under a loan agreement or line of credit from the U.S. Treasury under the Economic Stabilization Act of 2008 that is intended to "result in a rationalization of the costs, capitalization, and capacity with respect to the manufacturing workforce of, and suppliers to, the taxpayer and its subsidiaries." This waiver of the limitation is not available if after the ownership change any person (including related persons, but excluding a voluntary employee's beneficiary association) owns more than fifty percent of the voting control or value of the stock of the old loss corporation.

Prior to the 2009 enactment of § 382(n), the Treasury Department and IRS had issued several notices which, in effect, voided the application of § 382 with respect to corporations that received bail-out funds under the economic stimulus packages. Notice 2008-83, 2008-42 I.R.B. 905; Notice 2008-100, 2008-44 I.R.B. 1081; Notice 2009-14, 2009-7 I.R.B. 516; and Notice 2008-101, 2008-44 I.R.B. 1082. There was some question whether these administrative actions were taken with adequate legislative authority.